You're More than Enough

Has anyone told you?

You're More than Enough

Owning your purpose

Armani White

You're More Than Enough by Armani White

Copyright © 2018 by Armani White.

All Rights Reserved.

ISBN-13: 978-0692142172

ISBN-10: 0692142177

Printed in the United States of America.

All rights reserved. No part of this publication may be reproduced, stored in a retrieval system, or transmitted in any form or by any means – electronic, mechanical, photocopy, recording, scanning or otherwise – without the prior written consent of the publisher, except by provided by the United States of America copyright law.

Scriptures quotation are taken from the New King James Version®. ©1982 by Thomas Nelson. Used by permission. All rights reserved.

Definitions are taken from Dictionary.com Unabridged, Based on the Random House Unabridged Dictionary, © Random House, Inc. 2018

ALL RIGHTS RESERVED

Printed in the U.S.

Table of Contents

Acknowledgments vii

Introduction xi

1 | Keep Your Covering 15

2 | Identify 27

3 | Seeds of Love 39

4 | While You Wait 51

5 | Joy 67

6 | To Cultivate Peace 79

7 | Peace Is Given to Protect 89

8 | Fulfillment 101

9 | Fire 111

10 | You're More Than Enough 131

Closing 141

Acknowledgments

"Giving thanks and honor where it's due."

— *Armani W.*

<u>Heavenly Father – My Abba</u>

First and foremost, I want to give all thanks and glory to the Most High God, Jesus Christ. Lord, I thank you for allowing me to embark on this journey with You. Thank you for never letting my hand or heart go.

You are genuinely a Father to the fatherless and a Comforter to the lost. For that, I thank and love You. Father, I promise to continue to keep my mind, body, and soul pure before you. I vow to always testify to your Great name. My promise symbol is my daily reminder to see myself the way You see me. I know I've fallen short of seeing myself as more than enough, so I promise to keep my identity in you and you alone. The flowers that You've given me let me know that in You, I am fearfully and wonderfully made. Jehovah, oh relational Father, I love You!

Davie – My Rock and My Foundation, a.k.a. Mom

Mom, I love you, and I thank you for always putting your best foot forward. I thank you that even in all your imperfections, you're perfect. You're always there, even when we as children fail to see your hand guiding us. I'm sure I can speak for my siblings and me, that we are forever grateful for you. Without you, we would truly be lost. You're our earthly angel sent on assignment to nurture and care for us. Mom, I thank you for always loving me and nurturing me whole. I love you, Mommy White!

Virtue – Armani (Dear Future Me)

Armani Girl, many years from now you are going to be glad you finally took the leap and published your first book. I'm proud of you. You've resisted the gravitational pull, and you are not going back to whom you used to be. I'm am forever grateful that you've used this moment to be vulnerable enough to write this book. I'm sure you'll look back and read this for the umpteenth time and grow to learn and realize that despite all your flaws, shortcomings, and setbacks, You're More Than Enough. Continue to be the best version of yourself, and let nothing nor anyone dim your light. Let your light shine before all men so that all who see will glorify your Father in Heaven.

<u>*My Brothers,*</u>

All of you are special! I love each and every one of you guys, from the oldest to the youngest. You all know how to turn a dull moment into a joyous occasion. From the jokes of Malique to the voice of Ahmed and the bizarre stories from Jermell, you guys sure know how to bring life into any given situation. My prayers for you guys are that you'll learn to love God unconditionally and never depart from His doctrines or His teachings, nor Momma's instructions. I love all of you! Never stop fighting to become your best self. Know that you're more than enough and there's purpose within you that's waiting to come out! Live life to the fullest knowing that God thought you are to die for! I love you!

<u>*Pastors*</u>

Pastor Yvette and Pastor Phillip, I thank you for all the teachings you've bestowed upon me. I honestly don't think you know how much you guys have loved me whole. I am forever grateful that I have the both of you as my go-to pastors and mentors. Thank you! You've taken a shy, timid, fearful girl and helped transform her into a firecracker—a force to be reckoned with! Thank you! I love you!

To My Readers

Dear readers, my prayer and hope are that you become whole and free as you embark on this journey with me. I want you to know that you're more than enough. Your growth, maturity and purpose are far too important not to take the time and invest in your soul. Never allow anything or anyone to define your destiny, your worth, or your value. Sit at the Father's feet and let Him love you whole, knowing that you are more than enough—you are to die for!

Introduction

"To be established in the truth of God while having the strength to deny every opposing word that is keeping you from your full potential."

— Armani W.

Watching the lovely lady holding her daughter's face made me cringe as she forced her to identify the beauty in her reflection. I was beyond hurt and saddened, to say the least. The expression on the mother's face was indeed a reflection of a mother's heart. She desperately fought to find words to reassure her daughter of her beauty. There was a moment when she glanced at me. I knew in my heart that her eyes were pleading with my soul to agree. I couldn't speak. As I watched the two, I myself was baffled, lost for words. I too was anxiously waiting for the response of the young girl.

She was gorgeous. Everything about her was beautiful. As I waited for her answer, I couldn't help but watch the tears stream down her face; her cry made my heart ache. I started to ask her for her name, but figured I'd do more damage than good. Just when I brushed that thought aside, I saw movement. This young girl called herself "pretty" and topped it off with pulling that "pretty" apart with words of shame.

Her "pretty" quickly turned into the nitpicking of her flaws. You could tell whatever lie nestled deep within her heart had taken root within her soul. Though she was gorgeous, she struggled with confidently calling herself pretty. It's a shame that she had a soul struggle, due to what she thought was flawed. If only she knew she is packaged that way, perfectly flawed.

It's crazy how much life can lie on you. Life has a way of ripping your beautiful soul out. It makes you think the very skin God placed you in was a mistake. God makes no errors: everything you are, everything you go through, and everything God has placed inside of you has a purpose. You're more than enough to let the lie and trickery of both this world and the devil paralyze you from becoming your best self. Be graced and know that God thought you were to die for.

Going back to the young girl, I'm not sure if it was a win or not for her that day. The expression on her mother's face and her sigh were one with a sense of relief that was buried in hope.

Honestly, I believe this mother has her work cut out for her. However, I pray this young girl sees that beauty is not only what you see, but it's also what's inside.

After I left that scene, many thoughts were running through my head. The first, what was her name? The second, how long had she been living in that mental state? Lastly, why couldn't she see she was beautiful?

Sadly, many souls are or were once like the one I encountered: lacking the real knowledge and understanding that they're more than enough. The way you were created is the way God intended! Oh, how I wish I could reach every lost soul, hug them, and tell them *they are more than enough.* Especially, the young child I encountered. If only she knew her worth.

I'm pretty sure somewhere along her lifeline the young girl was full of self-love, confidence, life, and beauty that exudes from the inside to match her outside. I'm not entirely sure what took place to cause the deep level of insecurity she now displayed, but I know one thing for sure. The moment this girl gets a grasp of knowing she is more than enough, she will be a force to be reckoned with.

I wrote this book for her. I meticulously composed an outline of what I knew would be beneficial for her soul, her spirit, and her future. I also wrote this book for you! I truly believe that you are to move forward in life. To do so, you first need to know your worth and who you are. As I sit here writing, I have something to say to both you and that young girl . . .

"What is your name? You ARE beautiful!"

1 | Keep Your Covering

One thing I know to be true is this: *"Honor your father and mother, which is the first commandment with promise."*

Ephesians 6:1

Childhood Daze

In 1998, running the block of Washington Ave., there were a bunch of us, ages five to thirteen. We stayed out late playing hopscotch, double dutch, tag, and hot peas and butter. The world was ours! You couldn't tell us nothing, especially after a fresh perm or a press and curl. Man, that childhood daze. I know you remember, jumping on beds and playing hide and seek (*innocently*). Yeah, I bet you were relentless and rambunctious!

Gosh, I recall at the age of seven my mother taught me how to take the metro across the boroughs. Back in those days, that wasn't considered dangerous. It was common. I already had my share of grocery shopping, as I casually went to the bodega around the corner. After shopping I would scream toward the window checking to see if my friends could come and play.

One day, I was so consumed with enjoying life, that I lost track of time. I was drawing on the cement with chalk, when I saw my mother frantically running toward me. Excitedly, I ran toward her, not realizing she was fuming. As I approached my mother, she wailed with fear and concern. She was upset, nervous, and afraid that I was unsupervised and out so late. At the time, I couldn't understand the issue; this was the norm for me. Little did I know the world I was in would soon diminish.

Times were changing, and I was getting older. What was once considered innocent play turned into kids being snatched, killed, molested, and harmed. I soon learned that my mother's concerns projected a line of protection. She, being my covering, protector, parent, and mother, knew something I didn't. Life as I once knew it in my childlike innocence and faith was changing. As a parent, she needed to correct her child. Even in all my innocence, she made every effort to protect my purpose, purity, and peace.

Line of Protection

Often, when we're growing up, we experience the fullness of our parents. We feel the rage, love, concern, chastisement, rebuke, support, and care. Combined, all our parents' emotions and actions are a line of protection. They know this is necessary to prevent us from experiencing the fullness of this world.

This world, when it gets a hold of you, snatches, taints, and destroys every ounce of possibility, purpose, purity, and faith you may have as a child. Scriptures like Psalms 127:3-4, Proverbs 22:6, and Matthew 18:2-6 show us that God cherishes children. Their faith, their love, and their innocence are pleasing to God. Just look at a child: It does not matter how many times they've fallen or gotten hurt, or how many times you told them no. Somewhere in their mind, they know that should they be persistent enough, should they try hard enough, should they get up one more time, there's glory on the other side.

The Lord God wants the same thing for us. He wants us to dare to love, dare to try, and dare to get up. Therefore, He sent us parents, guardians, mentors, and whomever else will keep us accountable. Our purpose and our potential are relying on our ability to get back up when the world knocks us down. To keep fighting when rejections come our way. To keep loving ourselves even when it seems as if it's nearly impossible.

Our Father, who is in Heaven, strategically created you from parents who are to cover you and guide you, so you can walk into the fullness of whom God created you to be. Every person to enter your life has purpose. Your parents or spiritual guidance is placed to cover you and guide you as you fulfill the very thing God created you to be.

<u>*Childlike Innocence*</u>

There was a time in my career when I was a family child-care provider. Apart from moments when the children drove me up the wall, there were many times when I would watch them and observe the freeing, relentless, and joyful countenance they carried. Every child under my care exuded a high level of innocence and love . . . as they should!

As I cared for these children, there was an automatic response from me. As an adult, currently without a child, I carried a sense of parental protection with urgency. Naturally, I would shelter and watch over these children. I cautiously watched to protect them from any potential harm or threats. This automatic parental response even spilled over to my siblings, from the eldest to the youngest.

I believe it was around this time when I understood my mother's frantic concern when I was playing late. A parent's central role and responsibilities are to nurture their child, educate their child, and protect their child at any and all costs.

As children and adults, it can be a bit tough to comprehend the role of a parent. Many of our difficulties come from our desire to grow, mature, and live life as we've dreamed and envisioned. When it came to the children under my care, I noticed they exuded this same desire, even at the age of two.

Watching the children freely be themselves took me back to a moment of my childhood. I was so full of joy and excitement; everything was new to me. All I knew was that I was supposed to have fun and live the life I was so full of. It was in that pivotal second when I understood scripture from a deeper perspective. I saw why Jesus cherishes children and instructs us to have childlike faith. I also realized why Jesus urges us to correct our children, and how, in doing so, it shows love. It's clear Jesus's teachings are full of purpose.

Childlike Faith

Do you remember when you were young, you wanted to become the most outlandish and most astronomical thing in the world? I bet your wildest dream was to become a lawyer, an astronaut, a doctor, an author, or own your own multimillion-dollar company. Mine was to own a hair salon and a restaurant all in the same building. I also wanted to write novels and other forms of books, until I realized reading and writing were not my strong point. So that desire quickly faded! (And now look at me!) What was yours? What is that childhood dream that is nestled in the back of your memory that you thought was too foolish to attain?

Somehow, as children, we dared to dream. We were not afraid to become our best self. Money was not a consideration, boundaries were without limits, and fear was unknown. God cherishes those precious moments, and He desires to bring you back into that same relentless feisty personality that will stop at nothing to fulfill your wildest dreams.

That childlike faith is what God honors. He urges children to come to Him. He knows they are without the burdens of the world. He knows that though life has knocked them down, they are still determined to learn how to walk. Though they've been scolded, they'll always love you like crazy. That faith, that drive, that determination is what drives God crazy about you.

Crazy Faith

So, one of my younger brothers went off to college a few years ago. When I say he picked the most expensive and furthest school you can think of, I mean he had no boundaries with his selection. Just thinking about his tab makes me cringe. Anyway, during his college selection phase there came a time when my mother sat him down and forced him to identify what he wanted. The thought of his desires scared him. He figured, (1) the school is too expensive and (2) the school is across the country.

My mother pushed him. And in his childlike faith, he went for it. Money was no longer an issue, and the distance was closer than we realized. My brother put everything he had into his desired school only to find out his wildest dream came true. He was accepted into his number-one choice. Not only was he admitted, but he also got a full ride! That's over $300,000 in college tuition paid in full.

Had it not been for Mom's relentless pursuit to push him, he would not have had that crazy faith to speak his wildest dream. The moment he confessed his heart's desires was the moment God was able to move mountains through his faith. Literally! Your childlike faith is what's going to shift you into another hemisphere. Dare to dream. Go back to those moments where any and everything was possible.

I know life has a way of deterring you from your hopes and dreams, but you must hold on and pursue your purpose with a passion. Right now, I want you to take a moment: grab a sheet of paper and a pen. Write down your wildest dreams. Be detailed. Be honest. Be in full expectation of what your heart's desires are.

Once you've finished writing down your wildest dreams, write down which one of those dreams you would like to accomplish within the year. Next, break it down into the next steps you must take within the next six months to achieve this dream. Once you've jotted down every detail and idea, look at your next thirty days. What will you accomplish from your six-month goal/dreams in thirty days? Hone into your thirty-day mark, and use it as a blueprint as you proceed into your next seven days of your life.

Make every day intentional. Dare to dream, have childlike faith. Remember, a dream without a plan is a dream that is not in God's hand. Give the Lord something to work with. Bring that childlike faith back to life! Live in crazy faith.

<u>Correct Your Child</u>

When God formed us, he created us with a host of dreams, desires, and goals. In His image, there are endless possibilities. Your childlike faith is what connects you to freedom and opportunities that are attached to your name in Him. Go figure; He urges parents to correct and scold their children. Not for harm, but rather for correction, guidance, and reproof.

That moment where I was scolded for innocently playing was my mother correcting me to protect me. She knew my eyes were not privy to the cares of this world. In her own strength, she did what she knew would be best to correct and caution me. Had it not been for the scolding, I would have continued to play all hours of the night. This would leave access to potential harm. However, due to her chastisement, I became aware. In her correction, I corrected my behavior.

Correction is needed. It may not always feel good or viable, but it's needed. This world has a way of removing and tainting your childlike faith. It has letdowns, disappointment, rejection, betrayal, love lost, danger, and many other factors. Due to your circumstances, your childlike faith shifts. As a result, you depict an image and character that resembles your journey. God desires you to live your fullest potential, so you need correcting. From parental to spiritual guidance, the Lord has placed people in your court to repair and restore your childlike faith.

Parental Correction

When it comes to your parents, no one knows you better than they do. They know your ins and outs. They know all fifty-nine of your moods, and yet they still love you. Your continual efforts to keep them out will not keep their love from you. Your parents, whether mom, dad, or both, are a representation of the Love of your Heavenly Father, here on earth. Your parents were divinely assigned to you, by God.

Because you were created with a host of endless potential, the Lord blessed you with parents that are assigned to use their "rod" in hopes of guiding and keeping you moving in the direction you ought to go. Now, I don't want you to look at the term *rod* as in spanking or beating, though in some cases that's needed. Let's look at *rod* as more of a measuring stick, guidance, or direction. Our parents are reinforcers of faith. They keep us on track to fulling and becoming our best selves. They're always pushing us and speaking life into us. When the world says you can't, your parents are right there rooting and cheering you on.

There are many who no longer have their parents, or even have parents who neglected them. It's unfortunate, but if that is the case for you, you must still see the beauty in your parents' existence. God sent your parents, mentor, or guardian of some sort to cover and watch over you. It's up to you to see the good and the potential and learn the lessons they bestowed upon you. Every situation has a silver lining. It doesn't matter if you think you have the greatest or worst parents. Choose today to see that God graced you with such parents to nurture you, teach you, and become a representative of His love here on earth.

Spiritual Guidance

Ephesians 6:1-2 tells us to honor our parents. It also tells us to obey our parents in the "Lord." Our parents in the Lord are our spiritual parents, mentors, teachers, and pastor. Our spiritual leaders are also here on assignment to guide and direct us to the Lord. While we have our earthly covering, we also need our spiritual covering. These spiritual teachers are to train and build us in our spiritual stature.

God has orchestrated an army of instructors and correctors that are in place to feed us spiritually and to guide and watch over us. Our soul matters to the Lord. Our Heavenly Father knows that as we grow and mature, we tend to pick up and develop traits that are not our own. Therefore, both our spiritual and earthly parents are placed to help restore us back to our original state. As we develop into our divine purpose, our parents are there to assist, carry, and cover us.

Our parents go through hell and back to tend and nurture us. Whether it's at home or on the pulpit, the number of battles and the warfare they endure to have a sound mind so we as the receivers are continually growing and maturing, is one steep price to pay. Do me a favor: when you visit your parents or the next time you're in service or meeting with your mentor, thank them. Give them the appreciation that is due. Whether you realize it or not, your purpose is attached to their direction, rebuke, and reproof. They are your covering!

Because of them your purpose and your childlike faith now have a fighting chance at becoming all that you've envisioned and, most importantly, all that God has called you to be. You're more than enough. Embrace your guidance and acknowledge them as they guide, nurture, and restore you to the very image God has drawn for you.

My Prayer

Father God, in the name of Jesus, I pray right now over your child. I pray that you allow them to see themselves in the same image you've destined for them. Allow their faith to be ignited in such a way that they will go for the very thing that you have placed within them. Open their eyes to their physical and spiritual parents. Allow them to know that they are divinely sent to them by you! Lord God, I ask that you cover your child in Jesus's name, amen ♥

Mission: Find out who in your corner you can call mentor, parent, or pastor. Take the time and be intentional about taking heed to their instructions. Take the good and learn from it!

** Use wisdom and pray for guidance.

2 | Identify

One thing I know to be true is this: *"For the Lord your God is a consuming fire, a jealous God."*
Deuteronomy 4:24

That One Sunday Morning

That one time at church it seemed as if everyone vanished, and I was left stranded, one-on-one, with the voice of my pastor's preaching, echoing within the depths of my blockage. It almost seemed as if Jesus Himself came down to orchestrate such an event—He did—causing the daunting thoughts of my past to rear their ugly head to face me. I couldn't believe this was happening. There was no place to hide, so I would have to face the very thing that I'd been masking. I would soon learn that day at church would forever change me.

My pastor preached on *the mask we wear*. It started out as a good sermon; we were hooting and hollering and saying, "You betta preach, pastah!" I was going along with the shouting, until his words hit like a double-edged sword. At one point during the service, uncontrollable tears started streaming down my face. Everything that my pastor preached on was correct for me.

If you asked me what was said, I would have no clue. My flesh missed the service, but my spirit caught every minute of the word. There was no more hiding. I had to face my fact: I was so strong yet so weak. I had done an excellent job at hiding the countenance of my heart. I was hurt and dragging that past hurt. Somehow, I learned how to mask my feelings, mask my situations, and project an identity of one that protected the pain I was feeling.

Here I was, well into my adult age, carrying past hurt and experiences that shaped me into the person I was. That wasn't me. I simply wore a mask to cover up my experiences. In my pain, I'd adopted a mask, which I had no idea was still on, let alone how to remove it. The saddest thing about our experiences is not that we've experienced them, but instead that we're unaware that we're still living with them. In life, what we experience is supposed to shape us and build our character, not change our identity. The way the Father created you was intended for you to evolve into whom you were designed to be. Not morph into something or someone else.

Masked and Marked

October 31 is the day many individuals feel safe enough to morph into their imagination. They dress up, wear weird clothing, wear all shades of makeup, collect items from strangers, and even come out during the darkest hour. They're masked yet marked with everything that screams "HELP ME, I'M LOST!" The identity of these individuals is concealed, yet the substance of who they truly are and what they relate to is revealed!

Funny, it doesn't take a national holiday to identify the masked and marked. They're hiding in plain daylight. The only problem is, they're not hiding from everyone else. They're hiding from themselves. You're masked, and you don't even realize it. Don't hide from yourself; make room for your growth. In this section we'll briefly touch on five points that will help you identify if you're masked and marked, as well as how to unveil your identity.

The five points that identify if someone is masked and marked are as follows:

1. They dress up.

2. They wear weird clothing.

3. They wear all shades of makeup.

4. They collect items from strangers.

5. They come out in the darkest hour.

Point #1. As a masked and marked individual, you may not have a clue you've dressed up in something other than what God clothed you in. However, what you do know is that you've dealt with some level of trauma that has lingered with you. There is so much more to you than what meets the eye. As you sit here, there is so much potential that wants to ooze out of you.

Point #2. As a masked and marked individual, typically, you're surrounded by individuals and situations that have no place in your future nor your purpose. Somehow you can't seem to understand why you attract weird company. Hint: It's your clothing!

Point #3. As a masked and marked individual, you're very colorful! You have a lot of skill traits, and your hand is in everything. This may not be a detriment. But indecisiveness and the inability to grasp one thing can prove to be a challenge for you.

Point #4. As a masked and marked individual, you morph into your surroundings. You feed into what others are giving you, and you conform to your company and environment. You're a chameleon.

Point #5. As a masked and marked individual, you experience many dark moments that you are unable to fathom, grasp, or come out of fully.

As a masked and marked individual, you may identify with some or all points given. Please note these points are not the only points, only what I'm touching on. Being an individual who is masked and marked is tough. Believe me, I know. You have no idea how many layers of masks you're wearing. However, the thing about masks is that they do come off. The first thing is seeing yourself as more than enough. You must be willing to partner with your healing, restoration, and the unveiling of your identity. If you're not ready, no worries; you're marked, so the mask is bound to come off, be revealed, or be stripped in some shape or form.

The Thing about Identity

Identity, to the Father, is important. God recognizes how He made you. When Adam and Eve were in the Garden of Eden, they ate the forbidden fruit. (Their identity was morphed.) As God appeared to them, God called out and said, "Where are you?" (Gen. 3:9). Not because He had no clue where they were. He's God; He knew their location. He asked, "Where are you?" because the appearance of their nakedness shaped their idea of how they perceived themselves, thus causing them to hide behind something God did not clothe them in.

There are many times when we are exposed ourselves—our flaws, our lack, our insecurities, the way we were raised, and the way we're living. When exposure comes, shame comes in all its fullness. When God called Adam and Eve, it exposed their fear. They were ashamed and hiding because of what they'd done and the consequences they would be responsible for. However, once God found them, that is, revealed their insecurities, He clothed them properly. The Lord gave them garments he felt suited their identity.

<u>Damaged, but Still Good</u>

Find what you've been masking. Uncover thick layers of barriers. Ask God to identify who you're pretending to be. Then, ask God to show you who you are in His eyes. If you need to seek counseling, it's okay, get it! When God revealed Adam and Eve, He showed them who they were pretending to be. They were fearful, dressed in fig leaves, and unstable in their calling. When God revealed the hidden measures of their heart, they were vulnerable, scared, and uncovered.

♦♦

There's a price to pay for wearing masks. Unfortunately, being someone other than what God called you to be and clothed you in comes at a cost. When you wear foreign clothing, you attract serpents, flies, strays, and everything that pulls you away from God and your purpose. Like Adam and Eve, if you're unsure of yourself, you will attract serpents who have no purpose in your life but try to tell you your destiny. If you're uncertain about your calling, hold onto the last thing God told you to do and do not fall victim to lies, sneers, or distractions.

Failure to hold fast to God's Word will cost you time and creates barriers in your future and in the future of your generation to come. Your disobedience creates a host of generational curses and burdens. Press your ear against God's mouth and listen carefully to the people you're around and watch the environment you're placing yourself in. If you attract weird company, flee every chance you recognize it. Cleanse yourself with the Word of God and ask Him to renew you and restore you back to what He has placed inside of you.

Create and Camouflage

Being a jack of all trades is cool; being a master of none is dreadful. There was a time in my life when I realized I was good at almost everything I put my hands to. I was All Things Armani, yet I felt so unfulfilled. It got to the point where I took my hands off every single thing and cried at the feet of Jesus. I was fed up. I hated the fact that I was so colorful yet lacking luster and vibrancy in one color. It was time to remove my hats and master my purpose.

There comes a time when you may look around you and realize that everything you're doing has no divine purpose. Continue to look around. Allow those thoughts to arise. Being colorful and gifted in many areas may cause you to miss your mark at your purpose. First, learn how to master your purpose. Second, gradually add and incorporate other skills and desires you may have. God will gift you with many ideas, many gifts, many talents, and many skills. However, you may not be ordained to fulfill every one of those gifts. Instead, you may be called to umbrella, incorporate, or include those gifts under your one divine purpose.

For example, by trade, I'm a cosmetologist, a realtor, a childcare provider, and a tax preparer. I feel unfilled in those giftings individually. However, my purpose is in ministry. Under Rise Ministry Inc., I umbrella my giftings in such a way that I not only use my gifts but also use my gifts for service while bringing glory to Jesus! Don't throw away your gifts, but instead find your purpose and seek God on how to incorporate those gifts into your calling!

♦♦

It's vital that you allow God to show you your purpose and your identity. Should you neglect sitting at His feet and seeking His will, you may fall victim to your surroundings. It's crucial that you stay away from the serpent. Resist the devil.

Don't allow him to feed you lies and ideas on your identity, your purpose, and God's promises for you. Instead, invest your time in God. The longer you rest in God's presence, the stronger you'll be at knowing who you are and your worth. As you are strengthened, you are less likely to fall victim to your surroundings, or in my words, form into a chameleon.

♦ ♦

The hard and unforeseen part about being masked and marked is that you may experience many dark moments. You may be completely unsure of your purpose and your future and lack luster and hope. You may even slip into spells of depression, have suicidal thoughts, and entertain other dark thoughts that are contrary to God. Depending on how deep you may be, those thoughts may even sound viable. DO NOT, I repeat, DO NOT BELIEVE THEM! Bind them up in the blood of Jesus and continuously meditate on His word and on His thoughts concerning you.

You are not damaged goods! You may be damaged, bruised, or struggling, but you are still capable of repair. So hold onto God's Word. At times it may be hard to determine what God is saying about you, so dig deep and seek help! It's important that you know that you are not alone nor do you have to go at it alone. Whether you seek spiritual or professional counseling, go get it. God is for you, and He forever has His hands and loving arms around you.

Marked the Mask

When God found Adam and Eve, He not only marked what was masked, but He also called it out and redressed them. When you are masked, in God your mask is bound to be marked. He will mark that mask. He will pinpoint, expose, and reveal what you've masked and concealed. God is after your hidden things, He desires to make you whole. When God found Adam and Eve, He stripped them of their false-god-like clothing and dressed them in His garments.

Do yourself and God a favor: mark your mask! Adam did! When God found them, Adam told on himself. Adam cried out, "The woman whom You gave to be with me" (Gen. 3:12). This marked the fact that Adam was not fully strong in the authority that was given to him, and thus fell victim to other opinions and thoughts. This also identified Adam as not being fulfilled and satisfied with His portion. "The woman whom You gave to be with me." Adam wanted to find fault in the blessing of God. He partially marked his mask, while God uncovered the remaining.

When your soul cries out, your soul is revealing the mask you've worn. It reveals the contents of your heart and the burdens you've carried. But that's only what you can see, a fraction of what needs healing. God, when He hears your cry, tends to your entire soul. Adam and Eve only pointed to what was visible to them. God revealed what was hidden in plain sight. He marked that mask and dressed them properly. The fig leaves were not of God. Yet Adam and Eve had no clue.

They figured they'd dress themselves to be able to cope and adapt to their situation. What garment have you clothed yourself in? Have you protected your own heart by camouflaging your hurt and concealing your wounds? It's time to stop playing dress-up. God wants to make you whole. God is calling to clothe you. The fig leaves won't do. He desires to dress you in tunics of skin. You're more than enough. No need to wear a mask and clothing that does not belong to you. Identify the barriers and burdens that are keeping you from walking in your fullness. Your future is depending on you!

My Prayer

Dear Heavenly Father, Lord God, I ask that you help your child unveil the hidden things that are keeping their heart far from you. Lord, place them in your glory and search them in your garden. Father, I ask that you identify the very thing that needs healing so they can walk in wholeness. Assure your child that they are more than enough and their purpose is waiting for them. In your Son Jesus's name, I do pray, amen♥

Mission: Uncover your hidden truths. Ask the Lord to show you what you've hidden from Him. Then, ask Him to reveal your identity.

3 | Seeds of Love

One thing I know to be true is this: "There is no fear in love; but perfect love casts out fear, because fear involves torment."
1 John 4:18

True Love Will Wait

February 5, 2006, was the day I dedicated myself to keep my body pure until the day of my holy matrimony. The events surrounding that day were truly life changing! I went to a Spanish Encounter, and when I say there is no language barrier when it comes to the things of the Lord, there is none! That weekend wrecked me for the better! God had a tailormade message for me. He sent me a word that continues to minister to my soul, even after many years!

As I sit on my bed, I can't help but look at my wall thanking Jesus. On my wall, there's a tannish-orangy, old-looking, wrinkled, scroll-like paper hanging from a thumbtack. This "Promise Pact" paper was originally dated, signed, and witnessed at that Encounter. The title, in bold lettering, reads: *True Love Will Wait*. A real badge of honor!

At one point in my life, the testimony of this Promise made me cringe. It confessed what I feared admitting: I had not waited. Whenever I randomly came across this pact in my room, I hid it or intentionally lost it. I prayed that the evidence of the truth would magically vanish. It didn't. I moved about three times after that Encounter; you would think that somehow that Promise Pact would get lost or destroyed. However, someway, somehow, this *paper* kept surfacing.

Must true love *really* wait? Not fully understanding the depths of the pact's message, I questioned its purpose and neglected the promises I once made. I would love to paint the picture that I waited for matrimony, but let's be honest, that was not my portion. Now, though, I smile at my wall because something that once made me cringe is now a badge of honor—knowing that Christ is a redeemer of time and has redeemed what I've lost.

Graciously, what was initially signed and dated back in 2006, was resigned and recommitted in 2014. I would love to say it's been an easy and patient journey. But there were many moments where I felt unease, picked over, and forgotten. I didn't want to wait; love was taking a long time. I'd always envisioned myself meeting love at this "special" age and making my way down the aisle in the proceeding years after. It didn't work like that. I had to realize that love as True Love is more than that.

The Constant of Love

Love as it has been painted for us should be repainted. The story of love that has been painted, so neatly depicts an image of a happy-go-lucky fairy tale where a princess finally meets her prince charming, clothed in a suit of armor. In a narrative, that is what love is like. However, true love, as we grow to realize, is a bloody, sin-filled death. Surely love is to lay its life down, a real sacrifice and gift for the receiver. "Greater love has no one than this, than to lay down one's life for his friend" (John 15:13).

The constant of love is presented in a sacrifice. It is a sacrifice so holy and pure, yet so submissive and serving. Love in its purest and fullest state is unconditional, removing conditions and boundaries which prohibit the real manifestation of Love. Love states that before you find love, you are to love yourself thoroughly and sincerely. We'll talk more about that in the next chapter.

Memories Ring a Bell

There were moments when I would reflect and think back to those times when I freely gave my body away. I gave my heart, time, and love that was intended to be set aside and labeled sacred in God's hands. As I would reflect, thoughts of shame, doubt, and insecurity would surface. Questions like, "Why was I so silly?" "Why could I not wait?" "How could I not know nor understand my worth?" or "Why was I so desperate?" would continuously flood my mind.

Isn't it funny how when you become a change agent for the Lord, the enemy instantly tries to remind you of your past? The devil tries to manipulate your mind into feeding you the complete opposite Words that God has called and spoken over you. Those memories that ring a bell, you must refute with the Word of Christ. The constant of Love does not remind you where you came from nor what you've done. The Word of God tells us that through HIS Word, we are "casting down arguments and every high thing that exalts itself against the knowledge of God, [while] bringing every thought into captivity to the obedience of Christ" (2 Cor. 10:4-5).

As quickly as those thoughts would come, they were hard for me to shake. Over time, I had to nurture my mind with the Word of God and allow my thought process to be renewed with the Spirit of God. It takes time. But you must be determined to feed your Spirit with God's Words. To the enemy, your mind is a battlefield, and that serpent will do anything to keep you from maturing in God's truth as you develop in His will.

The key is to keep speaking life over yourself. Whenever daunting words or thoughts creep in, snap back with the Word of God. Study His precepts and mark His Words on your heart! Here's a free tip: When thoughts that are contrary to what Christ calls flood my mind, I go to the Word of God. I find scriptures about what the Lord says about me. I meditate on them, write them on a sticky note or index card, and either place them on my wall, on my mirror, or in my journal! Whenever I feel a thought creep in, as a reminder, I head over to my prayer wall or journal and speak God's word back to myself.

Let's Grow Forward!

You know how everyone repeats catchy clichés like: "It is what it is," "Let go, and let God," "Forgive and forget," "Let it go," "Move past that," or, "Forget that it happened"? The truth of the matter is, while you're in the thick of things, those saying are just easier said than done! But . . . I think it's time for me to burst your bubble with just one more self-coined phase: **"Grow forward!"**

Unlike many sayings, "Grow forward," gives you a fighting chance to partner with the Holy Spirit in your self-healing and journey to love. When you're <u>growing</u>, you are stretching the limitations of the state in which you once were. To move <u>forward</u> is to acknowledge the journey you've been through and choose to take steps to get through what's been holding you back. Thus, you move forward in life.

When you combine the two, you are choosing not to allow your present or future state to be dictated by your former. At the same time, you are not disregarding nor sweeping under the rug your experiences or journey. But rather, you are taking your experiences and your journey as life lessons. These lessons will help develop you and catapult you in the direction God has mapped out for you.

Yes, at times, particular situations sting and linger a bit longer than others. The key is confession! Confess what's hindering you, speak it out, and acknowledge it. Don't allow those feelings to lie dormant. The moment you're able to speak and release them from your grip is the moment you give the authority back to Christ. In return, you now have a form of dominion over them. Your journey will be a testament to others who've experienced and been through similar situations as you.

Your experiences are not only for your future, but they're also for all who are willing to watch, learn, and grow from your life story as they are overcoming their own. Hint: *the purpose of this book*! The moment you grow forward from your life's journey is the moment you'll begin to give yourself a fighting chance. As you continue to grow forward, your self-dialogue and the image you have of yourself will be packed in such a way that your flaws and experiences will appear perfect not only in the eyes of Papa, but also in yours.

<u>Packaged Perfectly Flawed</u>

So, there are some who are aware that I've battled with eczema for practically my entire life. If you don't know me, it's cool; I'll give you the rundown. At the age of three, I developed eczema. Throughout my entire childhood, I was teased and questioned about the scarring it left on my body. Naturally, I became self-conscience—not because of my own thoughts, but rather, because of the daunting teasing I received from others. There were times in the scorching hot sun when I would wear long sleeves, jeans, and sweaters to cover my scars.

I soon realized I was putting myself in more agony than the hateful remarks were. I had to go on a journey of understanding that the way God packaged me was perfectly flawed. Does Christ want our bodies to be afflicted and outside of the original image He imagined for us? Of course not. However, the simple fact that God is God of all proves that your flaws and the cross you are carrying are no surprise to the Creator that predestined you.

Sure, our flaws and situations have a way of presenting themselves that make them seem as if they're the death of us. But you must see past that! You must come to the understanding that whatever your image, your unfair family circumstances, or even the short stick that life dealt you, God designed you fearfully and wonderfully. Your flaws and your uncontrollable predicament that appears as a flaw are perfect in the eyes of Christ. See yourself in the eyes of your Creator.

The longer you allow what you're staring at in the mirror to hinder you, the harder it is for you to hear God's one true Word concerning you. You are fearfully and WONDERFULLY made! You're more than enough. The moments when I regarded eczema as a mere flaw that was perfectly packaged, were moments where I was able to completely heal and use my scars as a testimony for those who are struggling with such afflictions.

Take ownership of who and how God created you. Allow the Spirit of Jesus to rest on you and remind you of your image. You are not the image of how the world views and labels you; you are the image God created you in. The Holy Spirit is there to bring all things to remembrance, including the thoughts Jehovah thinks toward you. As you continue your journey to love, remember that this journey will consist of you owning that you are beautifully flawed, packaged perfectly!

Planting Seeds of Love

It's vital that you continually plant God's words in your heart. It's effortless for us to believe the lies and the antics of the enemy. They seem convincing because, at times, they're circumstantial. They're based on our surroundings and look promising. However, they're not true! In some shape or form you've allowed the lies of the enemy to affect your love for yourself! The longer you feed into the lies the enemy has told you, the harder it is for you to realize the truth of God and His thoughts toward you. Believing lies creates an underlying level of self-hate or self-rejection.

Uproot those lies; backtrack to when you first believed you were not good enough. Take a second and think back to the time when you were ambitious and loving every part of yourself. Remember that person you used to be. Speak back to that child you once were, and replant those seeds of self-love. Go back to the very first time when your heart was violated. Take a moment and forgive your violator for stripping you of your precious innocence. Now, take a moment, and forgive yourself for not allowing yourself to grow forward in love. Give yourself a second chance at self-love.

Embrace the person God is shaping you to become. Rest on God's Word, knowing that in Him, there are plans of purpose, future, and hope. Know that God thinks good thoughts toward you. The Lord will not harm you, nor does He want you resting on what hurt you. Allow yourself to have a fighting chance to grow forward!

Total Substance

It's a given. God desires for us to find Love. For some, He also wants His Love to be shared with a spouse in holy matrimony. The journey to such love is rewarding, as long as you allow yourself to see and acknowledge His hand on your life throughout the entire process. As you go through this journey, it may seem vulnerable, intimidating, and mind-boggling, to say the least. However, continue to surrender your heart to Jesus and allow Him to expose every inner part that you've kept hidden due to shame.

Proverbs 3:9 tells us to, "honor the Lord with your possessions, and with the firstfruits of all your increase." When it comes to honoring the Lord with our possessions and our firstfruits, it first starts with you. He calls us a *living sacrifice*. So in conjunction with what we can tangibly give Him, He wants us to honor him in such a way that will require a living sacrifice. Learning how to love yourself entirely is a real sacrifice of letting those memories that ring the bell to your past die.

When you begin to plant seeds of His Word in your heart, you are allowing yourself to be that living sacrifice that is honoring the Lord with the possession of your heart. Submit that grasp that you're clinching so tightly, into the hands of

Jesus. You'll be freed to grow forward. As you grow forward, you'll grow to know and love that you're packaged perfectly flawed. Know that everything you are and everything in your circumstances is part of the perfect plan of God. Regardless of your flaws and your lack, God saw fit to use you for a greater purpose.

Giving your heart to Jesus is the total substance that God requires of you. He desires to restore you entirely so that you are whole and ready when it comes to finding true love. "'The two shall become one flesh'; so, then they are no longer two, but one flesh (Mark 10:8). These areas that I've touched on are just a taste of what God may be dealing with as you are either waiting on your journey to love or as you are strengthening your relationship with the one whom you love.

As you turn the next page, we are going to dig deeper into this thing called love! In my belief it's imperative to understand the purpose and meaning of love as you wait for love and as you are fulfilling your purpose.

My Prayer

Dear Heavenly Father, in Jesus name I do pray, and I exalt your Name. Father, I thank you and give you all the Glory! Lord, today I ask that you cleanse your child of every barrier and heartache that is preventing them from living their life whole and pure before you. Father, I pray that you embrace them with the Love of Jesus Christ and show and tell them how much they mean to you. Father, take them on the journey of self-love, as they are either waiting to find their true love or building their relationship with the one whom you've sent for them to love. Papa, I ask all this in your Son Jesus's name, amen ♥

Mission: Speak words of life and love into yourself. Rebuke the devil every time he calls you anything that you are not, and speak words of wisdom and life!

4 | While You Wait

One thing I know to be true is this: *"Wait on the Lord; Be of good courage, And He shall strengthen your heart; Wait, I say, on the Lord!"*

Psalm 27:14

Preparation of Love

There was a time in my life when I was utterly obsessed with the idea of marriage. It almost seemed as if every guy I met or knew, I questioned whether he'd be the one God had for me. I figured that since I'd dedicated my life to Christ, He was going to magically send my husband whenever I prayed. I soon realized God does NOT work in that fashion.

Along the course of this common obsession, Christ ministered to my spirit a few things that have helped mature and prepare me for the love He has for me. I know waiting for love can be extremely time-consuming. If you've already found love, I understand that being able to sustain your relationship as one that is honoring to Christ is very crucial for your matrimony. Therefore, I share three pointers with you. These pointers will help you along the course of your journey as they have helped with mine.

1. Love is unconditional, removing all conditions.
2. Love is submissive and serving.
3. Love is love, on top of what is loved.

Unconditionally Removing Conditions

If you're currently like me, you're still waiting for your Boaz, Paul, maybe David, or perhaps your Ruth, Deborah, or Sarah (whomever). This stage of your life can seem frustrating and feels like an eternity. I would like to think I am the first to tell you this: it does get easier! If you are currently waiting and are patiently waiting in Christ, keep waiting!

As I waited for Christ to align my footsteps leading to my spouse, He tore up every ounce of conditions that prohibited the real manifestation of what love looks like in my life. Currently, where I am right now in my life, I continuously bless the Lord for not answering the prayers for my husband to come forth in times past. I was not ready! *Whew, you would not catch me stating that a few years ago . . . or even months ago!*

Depending on where you are right now in your walk and relationship with Christ, first, some preparations must take place. The Word of God tells us to "present your bodies as a living sacrifice, one that is holy, acceptable to God which is your reasonable service" (Rom. 12:1). As a living vessel of the Lord, you will be used in a capacity that will exemplify our Savior in the fullest manner. You are an ambassador of the Lord, so everything you do and associate with will testify our King.

<u>*Inner Man / Heart*</u>

It's true, the Lord loves you unconditionally! However, part of the condition is that you are a changed agent in Him. Thus, He loves you unconditionally while removing the conditions that separate you from Him. There are many areas that the Lord may be dealing with you concerning your soul as you wait. We're only going to look at three. One, the Lord deals with your inner man, your heart that connects His Spirit to yours. Two, he deals with your thoughts that manifest in your actions. Three, he deals with lust and sexual sin.

Jeremiah 17:9 and 10 tells us, "The heart is deceitful above all things, and desperately wicked; who can know it? I the Lord, search the heart, I test the mind, even to give every man according to his ways according to the fruit of his doings."

Your heart in whole is what drives and dictates your actions. Thus, the Lord is continuously examining it to test your intentions. He is looking for a pure and genuine heart. One that will carry out His precepts yet is bold and willing to walk out His will courageously. Before the Lord will send you your spouse, your heart, intentions, and motives must be pure unto Him!

Cowardly "Humble" and Pure in Motives

Why is humble in quotations? Simple. Most of the times we as believers love God wholeheartedly, yet there are some barriers and limitations we have set for ourselves. Often, these barriers are hidden by what we call "humility." We give an appearance of walking humbly before the Lord and then hide behind Christ shivering when called by him to do something. *Ouch!* I know, I've been there; that's why I'm touching on it! When Moses gave the mandate to Joshua to carry on the torch (Joshua 1), there were two instructions: (1) Follow the Lord's commandments and love the Lord thy God, and (2) be courageous and strong!

When it comes to walking in the fullness of the Lord, it's imperative that you don't hide behind God, but instead step boldly to the throne of grace. Before I go any further, there is a time and a season when God will release you into your calling. However, many of us are stuck in times past, waiting on the

Lord. Yet, God has already called you, and He's simply waiting for you to act and move!

This is a matter of the heart. As you're stuck in your earlier calling, you are prolonging what God currently has for you. As a result, there will be some cleaning that must take place. For starters, know and trust that God has called you! There is no better you than you! If you must start over, that is okay. Give yourself a reset and a boost in your purpose. Affirm yourself in the Lord and get to work.

I want you to see yourself as more than enough. No longer will you hide behind God, but instead you will stand with God as He leads you. The moment you vouch for you is the moment Christ will begin and continue to work in you. *So does that mean He's not working in me now?* Of course not! It just means He's waiting for you to move and be secure in Him.

It might seem scary to launch out on faith, and that's okay. Faith is leaping and walking in that you cannot see, though you perceive it. As a child of Christ who has pure intentions for the Lord in everything you do, Abba wants to see you move! The Lord wants to see your light shine so all who see will honor Him in heaven. All your love and dedication to the Lord will not go in vain. The Heavens are backing you every step of your way! Encourage yourself in faith, get in the water, and allow His Holy Spirit to lead you!

Tip: God cannot order your steps if you refuse or are afraid to take any! Give God something to work with and show Him you're cut out for the job.

** *As you wait for love, allow the Father to teach you higher levels of confidence and boldness.*

<u>Proud and Noble</u>

The *proud and noble* are those who are hardcore for the Lord. However, somewhere along the line, they are subjective to pride. That's not so bad; it is fixable—if you're able to acknowledge or detect it. It's very easy to miss being proud and noble, especially when you exude a high level of drive and passion. However, most of the time, this can stem from a high level of rejection, opposition, or praise in areas of your life. Anyone can slip into this. Therefore, it's crucial for every follower of Christ to examine their motives and allow God to prick their heart.

God loves pricking our hearts. It shows Him that we are not deaf to His voice and that we are still able to receive what He's instructing. If you fall into the category of *proud and noble*, allow Christ to lead you back to Him. Allow the Father to humble you in areas in your life that need humbling. It's crucial that you keep a healthy balance of pouring out to others and receiving.

Tip: Often, when you are always pouring out into others, you promote a high demand for yourself. As a tip, guide them to Christ and additional resources. This will not take anything away from you, but rather add to your credibility while taking the load off.

***As you wait for love, allow the Father to teach you new levels of submission and honor.*

<u>Lost and Found</u>

When I say I had no idea I was lost when I was found, I mean I had no clue whatsoever! Most of the time, when we are lost, we are way off course from the direction God intended for us. This pertains to believers and nonbelievers alike. Those who are lost often need an identity shift. This shift is placing things back into their proper perspective, where God intends you to be. At times, this can be a bit troublesome to figure out.

However, it will require you going to the Lord and allowing yourself to be receptive to His voice as well as the voice of those He sends in your direction. A good indicator of how far you've strayed from God's path is whether you can receive constructive criticism and correct your course or you spend years on end in your life just walking around the same bush.

If you find yourself experiencing the latter, simply seek guidance and direction as to which area of your life God is going to remove you from as well as lead you into. This will require you to remove prior thoughts and inhibitions you once had. Having a renewed mind and allowing your spirit to be washed by His word will create a new birthing in you!

Tip: Just like it was for the children of Israel, the wilderness is no fun. However, every season promotes lessons. Choose to learn your lesson early. Pay attention to the attacks and setbacks. Those are indicators that growth is needed, and elevation is around the corner.

**As you wait for love, allow Christ to re-center you and guide you in the direction He desires you to go!

<u>Thoughts Manifest into Action</u>

As a man thinks, so is he. As vessels of the Lord, our thought process produces our outcome. Whatever you're wrestling with will consume you. There are times when we take the perspective of others or our own rationality and run with it. We believe what people think about us, the desires they place on us, and even what they envision as our purpose. Sadly, we even believe the lies the enemy has planted in our mind. As humans, we soak up everything that is given. This causes us to believe what is said to us or about us. On the contrary, these thoughts, ideas, or perspectives may not even be true.

However, our minds are constructed in such a way that we tend to project what we receive and perceive, onto our belief system. Due to our thought process, we hold firmly onto what we believe to be true. We somehow believe the lies of the enemy and trust other people's opinions and perspectives of our lives and future. This produces our thoughts, which manifest as our actions. If what we believe and think is outside of God's will, it creates chaos and confusion. This results in us being out of alignment with God's will.

It's crucial that you examine every thought to determine whether it's an opinion-projected thought, self-projected thought, or thought that is backed by physical and spiritual evidence. As you're Christ focused, your purpose will line up with His will. "Commit your works to the Lord, and your thoughts will be established" (Prov. 16:3). The Lord desires to sustain your mind, but you must commit it to Him. Understand that no matter how deep you are in your thoughts, your opinions, or your own will, if you seek the Lord, He will direct and establish you in Him. But you must be willing to turn your attention to Him.

Tip: God hears and leads all who call and go to Him. For God to direct you, you must resist your thinking, the pressures of others, and your own will, and submit to the Lord's directions.

**As you wait for love, allow Christ to fill your thought process with His love, wisdom, and precepts (word/doctrine).

Lust and Sexual Sin

I hear it all the time: "How do you do it?" One of the hardest things to do while waiting in the Lord is committing your mind, body, and soul to Christ. Fleeing from sexual sin and desires is not an easy task. Therefore, you must determine what's more important to you. Is it pleasing yourself? Or pleasing the Lord? If it's pleasing yourself, then you can stop reading right now. However, if you desire to please the Lord, then that's where you start!

The Lord God wants to know what's important to you. He searches our hearts seeking to give us our desires (Jer. 17:10). When it comes to lust and sexual sin, your heart must be in Him. God will deliver you from sexual sin. However, you play a role as well. You will be required to put in personal effort, such as keeping your eyes pure. If you know you get aroused by seeing specific images, choose not to partake in provocative movies or pictures. Further, watch the company you keep. Be mindful of being around the opposite sex. This is not to say you can't fellowship. You can; however, set boundaries. Don't stay out too late, and get off the phone when it hits that "hot" hour.

God gave us sexual desires, period. However, He desires us to partake in sex within holy matrimony. Every sexual act is a blood covenant. I won't go too deep in *this* book, but do know that each time you're intimate with someone, whether sexually, spiritually, or even by association, there are deposits and transfers of spirits that are being distributed with every interaction. Sex in the spirit realm is marriage. Each sexual act constitutes a marriage. Therefore, if you are not married to an individual, you should not be cutting the edge with sexual acts— mentally or physically.

Tip: Remaining sexually pure is challenging. If you need to, take a cold shower. Meditate on scriptures like 1 Corinthians 6:18-20. Ask for an accountability partner. Can't find one? *Reach out to me!* I will help you connect with someone who will help walk you through it!

**As you wait for love, allow Christ to love you whole while filling every burning desire with His love!

Submissive and Serving

Love is submissive and serving. When it comes to waiting for love, strengthen yourself in this area. NO! I did not curse at you! Submission is a mandate. Submission is serving. Learning how to love on others shows a level of love and care that you exude for both yourself and Christ. The Lord calls us to serve as unto Him. Serving, at times, can be a bit challenging. However, when you're married, your desires are no longer your own. When you're married, you commit to acts of service for the rest of your life.

I don't want you to think that if you submit, you are lower or less than. It's absolutely the opposite. When you submit, you show a level of compassion, humility, and control. Through submission, you become Christ-like, putting aside your desires and wants for the sake of fulfilling an ultimate purpose. You do this for the sake of unity, love, and supporting and strengthening others where it's needed. As you submit and serve, submission and servitude will come to you.

I do, however, want to encourage you as you strengthen yourself in the areas of submission and servitude. Remember, as you serve, your reward will not always come from man. Your reward will be reaped in heaven. I know you may be keeping tabs on your job well done. Don't—that's God's job. Submit that to Him. Allow Him to send you accolades and praise. In time, you will reap the benefits of your labor. In the meantime, hold on and keep sowing seeds of love while you wait.

Tip: Being submissive and serving can be hard. Use discernment, and balance yourself as you pour out. Keep Christ as your fuel; you don't want to burn out.

**As you wait for love, allow Christ to teach you how to submit and serve as unto Him!

<u>Love on Love</u>

Love. One whole person, loving on another whole person, through the love of Christ. As you wait for love, allow Christ to love you whole. Take time and evaluate where you currently are. Are you struggling with confidence? Do you rely on others to validate you? Have you identified your worth and your purpose? Do you know what it is that's keeping you from moving forward? Use this time and wait wisely. Take advantage of this moment, develop in self-love and maturity. Identify your barriers. Where are your shortcomings? Are you trying to build a life without first healing your heart or your soul? Are you walking with boldness and confidence in your calling and your purpose?

It's important that you take the time to ask and figure out these answers, as love is two whole persons coming together as one. In the spirit, two halves cannot make a whole; someone is bound to become damaged or impacted by the other's brokenness. You must know who you are. You cannot walk into a Godly relationship while you are still unsure about yourself, your calling, and your purpose. After all, a spouse is a helpmeet. How can your spouse help you meet your purpose if you lack certainty and clarity?

Use this moment to become full in the Lord. During this season, the Lord wants you to be completely vulnerable and secure in Him. This means He wants to build your confidence, your stature, and your faith. This season should be one where you search your identity in Him and Him alone. Use this moment to understand what it is that Christ will have you do. Use this as an opportunity to embrace your calling, your looks, your purpose, and your image.

Tip: Love on you!

**As you wait for love, allow Christ to tell you who you are in Him!*

My Testimony

In middle school, I had a Spanish best friend. She and I did everything together, so much one might think we were joined at the hip. Her church at the time was hosting a pre-teen Encounter, mentioned in the previous chapter. She didn't want to go alone, so she invited me. Looking back in hindsight, that event was one of the best things that could have ever taken place in my adolescence.

The Encounter was filled with so much love, freedom, and liberty. There was a time during a session where a Spanish-speaking minister held a pin-filled heart in her hands and with dancing and singing in the background, she started removing the pins, one by one. At the time I started bawling with uncontrollable tears streaming down my face. Those pins that were removed represented the burdens of life that I experienced at a young age. At that moment, God told me, "It's okay. I AM the restorer of every broken heart."

I didn't know it at the time, but that was the best illustration, one that I needed, and one I would carry with me into eternity. Truly that heart represented mine. By that time I had already experienced a lifetime worth of torment and spiritual battles that not even I was fully aware of.

Overall, that Encounter was worth a lifetime. The very last day the staff invited us to take a stand and oath of purity. They provided us with a promise pact and rings as a reminder to remain sexually pure until the day of our matrimony. I would love to say that I honored that vow I made to Christ, but in all honesty, I did not! Over the years I had my share of living and indulging in sexual sin. However, in March 2014, it all came to a halting stop.

I was in my last year of college when God called me back to purity. He'd called me numerous times prior to this date, and I responded with lip service—which my actions did not back up. This time, however, was different, and I felt it. Ironically, when Christ called me back into purity, the same promise letter I received and signed back in 2006, was with me in my campus dorm. I resigned it and prayed, and a few days later the Lord led me to a scripture that removed every ounce of sexual lust, thought, and desire. The scripture read: "Or do you not know that your body is the temple of the Holy Spirit who is in you, whom you have from God, and you are not your own?" (1 Cor. 6:19).

From that point on, my life drastically changed for the better. No longer was I half-heartedly following Christ. I was on FIRE. I pray that my testimony has inspired you in some way. I hope that you too will vow and continue to remain pure for the Lord. Purity is not just abstaining from sexual sin, though that's a significant chunk. Purity is honoring Christ with your entire body—your mind, your thoughts, and your actions.

<u>My Prayer</u>

Father God, in the Name of Jesus, I pray that you keep your child and cover them. Lord, I pray that you keep them pure at all costs. Father, I pray that you strengthen them as they wait for love or as they increase their love for you and their spouse. Father, help them to understand that in everything they do, they are to do as unto You. Father, I thank you for keeping your child. Lord, in Jesus's name I thank you, amen ♥

Mission: Embrace the season you're in. Ask the Lord to give you peace about working on you.

5 | Joy

One thing I know to be true is this: *"These things I have spoken to you, that My joy remain in you, and that your joy may be full."*
John 15:11

In the Fullness Thereof

Wheeeww, so this is literally a touchy topic for me. If I can be transparent for a moment, I promise my testimony will bless you in some shape or form. As we all know, life has a way of throwing curveballs that are in the form, size, and weight of fifty-pound bricks, and a whole house with the nine yards to match. Those curveballs have a way of robbing and snatching every ounce of joy that God has granted us. I will be the first to testify! As a result, I have struggled with joy and understanding the true meaning of it in the context of scriptures like John 15:11 and Galatians 5:22.

It would be foolish of us to think that just because we are followers of Christ or even doing better for ourselves that we would be totally free from hardships, letdowns, and struggles. The truth of the matter is that being in Christ does not exempt us. Being in fellowship allows us and grants us the tools to be able to grow forward and prepare for what's to come next. However, how we handle our journey and let it affect us solely relies on our strength, self-control, and trust in the Lord.

It has taken me a long time to understand this, and it's still a process walking in the fullness of this truth. Joy is not based on circumstances, happiness is. Happiness says, for this moment while things are working and happening for me, I delight in what is occurring for me, toward me, and around me. Joy, on the other hand, says, yes, I am full of life, but not the life that the world gives. Rather, full of life that can only come from the One true Creator, knowing that whether things are good or bad, my trust in the Lord will fail not!

Let's Be Honest

Okay, I'm glad we can be honest, because I wouldn't want it any other way. As I mentioned, life has a way of throwing some hard curveballs. Personally, I was dealt the shorter end of the stick, with expectations of being able to make up for my short end while supplying others where they lacked. From the inside looking out, I have always loved it! I enjoy being of service to others. I've always wanted to serve. However, I used to be unware of how to manage the weight.

While attempting to tend and cater to everyone, I lost myself. With high expectations of having to be everything to everyone, I forgot how to live, smile, and even laugh. At a young age, I carried burdens that were enough to measure a lifetime. Over time, what seemed to be operating out of pureness, turned into bitterness and a hardened heart. I became overly serious with everything, distant, and withdrawn, and became my own medicine. It only seemed right that since I was everything to everybody, I could be everything to me.

I played God with my life and hijacked the joy that was due me. Something that should have resulted in the act of service resulted in thick walls of barriers. I was in desperate need of help and had no idea. But because I'm in Christ, those walls and pretention were bound to come down. It does not matter how far along you are in your walk when you are in Him; He is going to deal with every ounce of you that has prevented His love from permeating into your life. That's what He did with me.

If you're in a predicament where the burden of life has weighed you down and snatched the joy out of you, in Christ, you're in luck. You are a child of God, and He desires you to live in Him at liberty. He will do everything in His power to chase the real you down! I told you, you're more than enough, and to God, you are just enough! The beauty of God is that while you are stuck in your ways, whether intentionally or not, He has a way of exposing, releasing, and mending the very thing that was one lost.

The Exposing

While we are stuck on yesterday, we build walls, masks, and an illusion of how we determine life to be, while missing the reality of what is happening right before our eyes. Those moments when I was a cross bearer started out in the fullness of joy. However, the enemy fed me lies, and I believed them, especially since the cross was getting heavy. To Christ, that's no excuse.

The measure of life that we're dealt, we're expected to carry. If we are not careful, we can allow our situations to justify our retaliation. In all honesty, to whom much is given, much is required. As God's warrior, he gifts you with measures that He knows will equip you and transform you for a higher purpose, but you must be apt to see it.

When we begin to drift into self-pity and self-sabotage, God will send messengers, nudges, and hints our way. However, because of the position of one's heart, those messengers can appear threating, judgmental, and out of order, especially when we look at what they're carrying. I know you've been there, throwing quotes and shade around like, "Only God can judge me," or, "Look at you. You got nerve!" "God knows my heart," and even those underlying seething thoughts when you're criticized or checked in what you're doing.

Measure of Offense

There's a measure of offense that comes when you are exposed! You know those air freshening commercials where someone walks into a room, and immediately they smell a foul stench, but the person that's been in the room the entire time has no idea what they're smelling? The longer a person remains in a room with a foul odor, the harder it is for them to detect it. The same goes for those who are carrying a load of mess that has completely thrown their entire countenance out of whack. When you are in the thick of things, you have no idea that you're out of order, out of position, and off balance. It takes someone walking into your life, to point it out and bring it to your attention.

Don't be offended. Instead, acknowledge what's been pointed out and work toward growing forward. I will be the first to say it is tough not to be offended and not to judge those who seem to be judging. However, here's a free tip: work on you! If you are honest with yourself, you could stand to have a few areas in your life tightened up. Who cares if the contents of your heart were pointed out by someone who seemed as if they have nothing together? Take the load off and count it as God himself pointed it out to instruct you on what needs to be addressed and changed.

Exposing is never pleasurable, but it's needed. There comes a time when we must face ourselves and submit what Christ has revealed into the hands of PAPA. Once we become truly honest and admit our faults, not looking at who pointed them out, we give God something He can work with.

The Releasing

Think of it like this: when an area of your life that needs to be addressed is picked and pointed out, you can release and submit it. On the other hand, had it not been exposed, you would not have had the knowledge or guts to release the very thing that hindered you. Exposing gives you the opportunity to release your grasp.

There are many times when I either noticed or was told that I was always serious with everything and should loosen up, smile, and laugh. (God is still dealing with me in this area.) My natural response was to become dismissive and offended. However, the more I allowed my heart to harden to constructive criticism, the longer I was in denial of what needed to change. Also, I became judgmental of others, as they pointed out something I was struggling in. I figured, who are they to judge?

There came a time when I had to sit at the feet of Jesus and begin to ask him to show me my heart instead of always pointing back at others. Surely, if multiple individuals pointed out the same thing, there must have been an underlying issue that God needed me to address.

Are you currently defensive at every instruction, suggestion, or feedback/criticism you receive? I know it may sting a bit, but it's important that you work in that area. Work hard at not being offended. Release that measure of offense to the Lord. How can you ever walk into the fullness of who you were created to be if you cannot mature in weak areas? The moment you own your faults while not placing blame back on others is the moment it becomes easier for you submit it at the feet of Jesus.

For practice: Whenever you feel a measure of offense rising, breathe, think twice, and think about what's being said. Ask yourself how you could benefit from what this individual is saying. How could you grow? What areas of your life, in your walk, could you stand to mature in? If you feel as if there are no areas that need work, kudos to you. However, still ask yourself those questions—growth is always necessary. Take the right advice, leave what does not pertain to you, and keep it pushing without the offense.

The release comes when you become completely honest with yourself, removing the offense and then submitting it into the hands of Jesus. Whatever the rooted cause of your outward appearance is, is where your offense will stem from. No one likes to be checked, corrected, or read. The truth hurts, but the truth also releases and sets you free.

The Mending

After the exposing and the releasing, it's time for mending. *Mending*, according to Dictionary.com is to "make (something broken, worn, torn, or otherwise damaged) whole, sound, or usable by repairing" or "to remove correct defects or errors in." Therefore, it's important for exposing and releasing to take place. You can't mend something if you have no idea what needs to be corrected.

In scripture, when a spirit (demon, bad habits) leaves an individual, that same spirit will come back to interrogate and take over your space as before. So if you've just been delivered from procrastination, those same spirits that are associated with procrastination will come back and tempt you again. However, after deliverance, most of the time a spirit will learn it cannot overtake you. As a result, that demon or bad habit will get stronger spirits to fight you down and prevent you from sustaining your deliverance (Luke 11:24-26).

The enemy knows that once you've been delivered, you're in a vulnerable state. So he'll do everything in his power to keep you from moving forward in life and your future. The adversary will send more of his flunkies to take you out. If you have not been mended, you can be overtaken.

In the process of mending, you're not only correcting and restoring, but also adding to and improving what's been lost or broken. Your deliverance and your pursuit of joy rely on you. What are you fueling on? What have you filled your spirit with? After you've been set free, you must put in godliness to prevent slipping back into where you've come from.

Submit your process to full joy at the feet of Jesus. Allow Him to reveal to you what needs to be mended, so you can walk in the fullness of Him. Become vulnerable before the Lord. Your healing and wholeness are solely dependent on you taking the steps to becoming your most fabulous self yet.

If you've been freed from depression, in conjunction with mending, you're going to fuel on joy. What does joy look like to you? Perhaps this means being intentional about spending quality time with friends and family. Go to a comedy show; laughter brings joy. Catch a movie, go to the park, try something new. Do something that you've never done before. Allow your juices to flow, and take partnership with the Holy Spirit as you are mended with Joy. Don't just sit there. Growing in the Spirit is a two-person job. Your work and your efforts are required, so get going!

Once you've fueled up on godly activities, you're filling that space that has just been cleaned. Now, when the enemy tries to take you and place you back into a depressing, fearful, or bitter state, he won't get ahold of you. You've learned how to live life after deliverance. You've learned how to "Submit to God. [And] resist the devil [so] he will flee" (James 4:7).

Pure Joy

You must know that you're more than enough than to allow past hurt, trauma, and shame to interfere with the person you are now transforming into. Make a declaration today! Promise yourself that every criticism you receive, every correction that is sent your way, you will neither get offended nor judgmental. But instead, you will use that as a tool to check your heart and figure which of its contents are causing the pricks from the chastisements that are received.

When it comes to joy, it is a fruit which requires cultivation. You must remind yourself of the Word of God whenever something comes into your mind and tries to rob you of the essence that is given by the Holy Spirit. There will be times when the results of the Words spoken over you will seem like less than what you have been planting. However, remain full of joy knowing that what you see does not dictate the amount of joy that has taken root within your soul.

It is the fullness of the Lord that is constantly working on the inside of you, so you too can experience Him in full joy. His love is taking root, and you will flourish in complete joy.

Gone are the days where you used to shrivel up in the offense. Now you will walk boldly as you evolve and mature into the exact image that God formed you in! Remember, the choice is yours. Choose today to live a life full of joy!

<u>My Prayer</u>

Father, in Jesus's name, Lord, I ask that you reveal the very contents of your child's heart. Expose every area that has robbed them of walking in the fullness of joy. Today, I declare that no longer will they walk in shame harboring the memories of their past. Lord, free them in Jesus's name. Search their heart and mend their soul and refresh them with your true Spiritual fruit of joy. Heavenly Father, I ask all of this in your Son Jesus's name, amen ♥

Mission: Today, I want you to laugh on purpose!

6 | To Cultivate Peace

One thing I know to be true is this: *"You will know them by their fruits."*
Matthew 7:16

It's so Spiritual

So, as you can see, and if you haven't noticed, these last few chapters are about the Fruit of the Spirit. For you to walk in the full knowledge of knowing that You're More Than Enough, you must have these seeds planted and cultivated, along with the remaining Fruit of the Spirit. Your journey in discovering self-love and living and the fullness of joy are two components that must take root in you and should be cultivated to continue to live in the fullness of it.

Peace is a fruit, which we will discuss in this chapter. However, peace is also a gift as well as a part of the armor of God; we'll explain that in detail in the next chapter. This is so important! Though peace is the same ingredient, like God, it functions in three ways. Having an understanding of how each function works will give you a vantage point. According to Ephesians 6:12, we wrestle not against flesh and blood. Therefore, the very thing that it is attacking your peace, confidence, and your ability to grasp the knowledge that you're more than enough is spiritual. Which means, this is a spiritual fight. You'll need to develop your spirit man, with Spiritual Fruit.

<u>But It's Fruit</u>

When the Holy Spirit came, He came bearing fruit and a boatload of gifts. It's the Holy Spirit's job to equip and sustain us for our journey as Christian believers. The Holy Spirit planted in us fruit that will show evidence of being a child of God. Gifts are without repentance and are given out of God's free will. The Fruit of the Spirit testifies we are of Christ and not of this world. Just like any other tree growing fruit, its seed must first be planted, rooted, and cultivated, before any evidence of produce.

To Be Planted

First things first, as a child of God, you must know the fruit of peace is yours! If you feel as if you're in a position where peace is not evident in your life, just ask! The Fruit of God is given liberally. He is not slack with providing fruit. You must know you're more than enough, and He desires you to live your best life with the fullness of peace. So the peace of God is planted in you!

The moment you decided to rededicate your life to Christ is the moment He sent your Helper, the Holy Spirit, to bear witness of you. The planting of peace already took place in you the moment you chose to walk in fellowship with God. However, just because the seed is planted does not mean it's in the proper environment to fully grow and produce its full purpose.

My Avocado

One of my favorite fruits is avocado, so one day I decided to grow an avocado. Before I go any further with this story, let me admit: this avocado never grew! Okay, now that that's off my chest, I can continue. I watched a bunch of videos and read a few articles on what the process of growing an avocado should be. After a few videos and a couple of articles, I thought I was an expert.

Every video and article told me to clean the avocado seed very well, peel off the outer layer, and place a toothpick on both sides of the seed. Once I finished, the easy part was to place the bottom part of the avocado inside of a cup filled with water. It's essential that the seed is not entirely immersed in water. I did everything to a T, following what I believed was correct; however, I yielded no results. I had the seed, but the seed was not adequately planted, and my results were void.

Many of us, like me with my failed experience, try to mimic what others are doing with their walk and expect to yield the same "fruitful" results. The will of God is not tailored like that. When it comes to the fruit of the Spirit, each and every one of us is given our portion of His Spirit, and it's up to us to seek Christ on how our seed ought to be tended to.

What Is Your Foundation?

Doing what videos and various articles instructed me, did produce roots. The process that I mimicked from others resulted in a sprout of **one** root! Should my avocado have a real chance at growing correctly, I would have to consult an expert, get educated, and watch the fruit of the educator's teaching. My learning and discipline would then take root and produce the evidence of what had been planted, rooted, and cultivated.

When it comes to your walk and your ability to adequately produce your God-given seed, you must allow the process of His planting to take place in your life. Watching various videos and reading articles are great. However, should you walk in the fullness of the Lord, what's greater is sitting at the Father's feet. Consult the Master Expert called the Holy Spirit. Seek Him with all diligence, get educated by His power and His disciples. Allow His will, love, and desire for you to be the foundation of what will take root in your soul.

The foundation of His love is what will allow His seed to be rooted in you! Without the proper foundation, you will have any and everything growing within. First, ask yourself, what is my foundation? What is my heart's desire? Is my heart's desire the love of Christ? Is my heart's desire the cares and activities of this world? It's vital that you answer truthfully. If you're unsure what your answers might be, look around you. What are you mainly consumed with? What you consume will show where your foundation is.

Your foundation is the determining factor of how your seed of peace will grow. Before a farmer plants, first, he tends to the ground that will sustain the seeds. He toils in the field: whacks out weeds, removes harmful bugs, and lays down fresh soil that will grant a cohesive environment for his seeds to grow. That's the same thing the Lord desires to do with you.

He desires to whack the weeds and cares of this world. The things that you are consumed with that will choke and eat His seed alive. The Lord God will remove harmful bugs and remove harmful individuals and situations that are placed and proving to be a hindrance to the maturity and growth in your walk. God is not negligent when it comes to the foundation of your soul. If you are in a situation where it seems as if everything you've ever planned for and expect to happen does not happen, and if it looks as if people are leaving left and right, trust God in your process. If you are walking for Him, He is merely removing weeds and taking you out of situations that no longer serve a purpose in your walk. He is clearing the foundation where His seeds are to take root.

To Be Rooted

The very foundation of your soul will determine how His glory will take root in you. As mentioned, if your spirit is in an environment where the produce of His Spirit cannot grow, God will remove everything that is stunting the growth of His glory that is planted in you. Should you walk in peace, you must be rooted in Him! Any other root won't do! Now that the foundation of Christ is laid, the Peace of His Spirit has a fighting chance of being rooted and cultivated in your life.

The rooting process allows your spirit to take root in His presence. Get intimate with the Father. Be intentional about building a relationship with our Lord and Savior. Don't settle for one root that videos and articles produce! Do the work and read His Word. Seek wise counsel. Meditate on who He is and what His Word Says. The root of the Father comes from your foundation being in Him. If you are not in Him, your roots will not gather in the direction of the Father.

The only way for peace to fully grow and produce in you is to be intentional about being rooted in Christ. The fruit of peace comes from the Holy Spirit and the Holy Spirit alone. Should you have the real manifestation of the Peace of our Lord, you must go the Father! In the beginning, it may seem hard and even feel weird. I get it: you may not hear anything that the Lord is saying, you may not understand what you are reading, and it will be frustrating when you do not see your desired growth. But you must continue to cultivate your spirit!

<u>To Be Cultivated:</u>

As you are taking root in the Father, it's crucial that you are not neglecting the fellowship of brothers (Heb. 10:25). Sure, alone, you can go far in your walk with Christ. But should you walk powerfully in Christ and walk in the fullness of Him, you need others! The increase of knowledge and your understanding will come from others. Your pastor, your mentor, your spiritual advisor, and your brothers and sisters in Christ all play a significant role in your comprehension and continued growth in your spiritual walk.

Cultivation is increased intentionality. When a farmer has planted on fertile ground, he doesn't just plant his seeds. He continues to do the work. The farmer does various rounds with his workers to ensure that the seeds he planted are growing correctly and are protected against any hurt, harm, or danger that pose a threat to the growing process. Even after there is evidence of fruit being produced, the farmer continues to do rounds, making sure the cultivation process of what he has planted is sustaining its purpose. What makes you think the Lord God does not want to continue working in you after He has planted His Spirit?

He desires to do continued work in you! It's a developmental process that needs continued cultivation. The peace of Christ comes with an increase of intentionality. You must be intentional about strengthening yourself when it comes to the peace of Christ. You'll need other like-minded believers around. Be intentional about being engulfed in the ways of God and not falling victim to the norms and customs of the world. It will take an ample amount of work. God will place an abundance of people and situations around you that will be used to refine and develop your fruit of peace.

About Development

A few years ago, I noticed I was struggling with being patient. Like peace, patience is a fruit (needs cultivation). My solution was to pray and fast asking the Lord to strengthen me in this area. However, immediately I noticed that the exact opposite took place. When I asked for patience, it seemed as if I developed more in frustration; I had a short fuse, I was agitated, and anything and everything annoyed me. So I kept praying and fasting. Over this repetitive cycle, God kept exposing areas where patience needed to be filled. Which meant, there was tons of work that needed to be done, to strengthen and develop in patience. As a result, everything that required uprooting surfaced to the top; the scorching took place.

When you make a sacrifice, your sacrifice is being burnt, and you have tons of residue left on the surface. That residue must be cleaned and removed before the actual blessing is placed before and inside of you. *You cannot put new wine into old wineskins, or the new wine will burst* (Matt. 9:17). If you're going to walk in the fullness of peace, everything inside of you that is hindering you from living in total peace must be removed. It's a developmental process that must take place so you can walk into the fullness of the peace of Christ.

To Be Produced

As you can see, it takes time for the produce of peace to thoroughly cultivate and produce in you. As you lay the foundation of God's will within your soul, you are allowing God's glory to take root in you! The only way for God's glory to take root is to have your foundation in Him. The beauty of Christ is that He gives liberally! He desires you to have His peace and to have His glory within you. So, He gives it! However, it's up to you to strengthen your spirit and your growth in the direction of His will.

When you are intentional about allowing His fruit to be cultivated within you, you are giving yourself a fighting chance at allowing His fruit to be produced in you! Real produce starts with you! Ask yourself, what are you doing to be intentional about allowing His fruit to grow within you? Faith without works is dead (James 2:26)! Fruit without cultivation is futile! Your production results in your cultivation!

My Prayer

Dear Heavenly Father, I pray that you arrest every hindering thought and action that is preventing your child from walking and living the in the fullness of Your perfect Peace. Lord God, I pray that you continue to do the planting work in your child that will bring cultivation and the manifestation of your Peace at will. Lord, I thank you for granting them the power and desire to walk in you. Heavenly Father, we thank you in Jesus's name, amen ♥

Mission: Meditate on the peace of God. Reject everything that is preventing you from walking in His full peace.

7 | Peace Is Given to Protect

One thing I know to be true is this: *"Peace I leave with you, My peace I give to you."*

John 14:27

Gift with a Purpose

Imagine having full authority, wisdom, and power on earth. The strength to reject sin, the authority to call forth unspoken promises. The wisdom of knowing when to speak and when to hold your tongue. Now, imagine needing strength to renew your peace after being tempted, trialed, and tested! You have stood the test of time over and over again. Yet even in all your glory, you are still in need of the gift of peace to continue and to endure.

Jesus, after being led into the wilderness to be tempted, trialed, and tested only to be induced and have His authority questioned, stood firm in all His power. Still, He needed the strength of His Heavenly angels. If I had to assume, I would say they affirmed Him with the gift and power of peace. Not that Jesus lacked any, but being tested and placed in a situation where your godhead is questioned will do a number on your mind.

Jesus gave the gift of peace. Not for our pleasure, but so we could stand when faced with numerous tribulations. In John 14:27, Jesus declares, "Peace I leave with you, My peace I give to you; Not as the world gives do I give to you. Let not your heart be troubled, neither let it be afraid." Peace is a gift with a purpose. When Jesus graced us the with the gift of peace, He told us not to be afraid, neither let our heart be troubled. Later, within the same passage, He further explained that the ruler of this world is coming, and he has nothing in Him.

To fully understand peace as a gift, we must first understand its purpose. Peace gifted is purposed for armor! Ephesians 6:15, demands us to shod our feet with the preparation of the gospel of *peace*. The gospel is the testimony of Jesus Christ. How is it that the testimony of Jesus Christ is what we ought to prepare ourselves with? The testimony of Jesus Christ is what equips us with the power of Peace. Jesus Christ *is* the gift of peace!

No other Man has borne the same burdens we bear or has been tested with the same temptations we're tested with. Jesus Christ was dealt our measure of pain, burdens, temptations, and everything we've been through, times a million. Still being fully God and fully Man, he had the power of peace knowing that His purpose of saving that which is lost was *more than enough*, so He endured and rested in peace. The gift of peace is our armor to all those who believe!

Obtaining Your Gift

I wish I could conjure up a pretty, cool formula on how to receive the gift of peace, but I can't! The gift of peace is yours. Jesus said, "My peace I give to you" (John 14:27). As a child of God, you have direct access to all that He has in His hands for you. It's just a matter of you obtaining what's yours. John 3:16, "whosoever believes in Him . . ." Belief, to God, is a massive deal! God operates on your faith. Your belief system is what drives God! Without the faith/belief in Jesus Christ, you lack faith/belief in God. Your peace comes with your belief!

"You Have to Believe God!"

One night, I was in my mother's room, and she was completely knocked out. I mean snoring and all. (I love you, Mamma.) As I was sitting there watching TV, I looked back at her to respond to something she said, until I realized she was sleep. While deep in her slumber, she said, "You have to believe

God." My response was "*What?* I do!" I was confused and puzzled why she, being completely unconscious, would make a statement like this. I figured, I love God, I go to church, I read my word, I study nights on end, and my worship is for real. I believe God.

It wasn't until two years after that statement that I understood that I did not believe in God as I declared. (*Ughh, I hate I even said that!*) I made powerful statements, declared prophecy, walked in power, spoke with wisdom, yet failed in belief! My actions, at times, matched my mouth. But my heart and my thoughts denied what was supposed to be confirmed! Have you ever had a situational recall where you automatically placed a situation or an individual in a category that you've previously experienced? Yes? Okay, cool we're on the same page. This is what I did, time and time again!

I placed situations and individuals in the same category as similar experiences. Mentally, I expected the same outcome, though I verbalized something different. My belief in what I professed did not match what I hoped for. In my heart, I wanted to expect something different, but I was so obsessed with the prior experience that I projected my obsession into the current situation. I had my mind affixed to everything but the perfect will of God. Because God is truth and every man a lie, the Bible tells us that as a man thinketh, so is he. Though I verbalized what my heart wanted, I did not believe it. My belief system or lack thereof manifested in the physical.

It's so Spiritual

God, in all His power, requires a vessel in which He can dwell. He chooses to set His Spirit in us, with the expectation of our belief in Him. You cannot serve fear and God. You cannot serve mammon and God. "Can two walk together unless they agreed?" (Amos 3:3). God does not fancy lip service while your heart is far from Him.

Should you do the will of God, you must have your heart toward God. Whoever you bless, God will bless. Whoever you curse, God will curse (Gen. 12:3). Whatever is bound on earth is bound in heaven. Whatever is loosed on earth is loosed in Heaven (Matt. 18:18). Your thoughts, words, and actions have weight in heaven. You must realize that whatever you do here, though we are a recipient of time, is done in Heaven!

If your belief is not aligned with what you expect to see in the spiritual and physical realm, you'll produce your belief. Your thought process is what brings the manifestation! Your complete peace is resting in your belief. If you're constantly doubtful, you'll produce your doubts. If your constantly fearful, you'll never reap the benefits of faith. If you're always second-guessing or questioning your decisions, you'll produce the fruit of indecisiveness, unsure in all your ways!

If you want to live in peace, change your thinking. Get ahold of your faith and trust God with all your heart! Not a fraction, but with your entire heart, trust Him. Your peace of mind is contingent upon knowing that God's will, will be done. This is not to say you will never have questions or thoughts or feel a bit apprehensive—you will. However, tap into that fruit of self-control and use it. Rebuke those thoughts that are contrary to the will of God, call the Devil a liar, have peace of mind, and believe GOD!

Moses—a man with a stutter, a man with anger, a man born into racial dissension, a rejected man, a man who could not possess the promise that God gave—was found righteous. Even with all his shortcomings, he was found blameless due to his belief. However, before Moses could obtain the gift of peace, he had to first reap the fruit of peace. He underwent a process that prepared him for the proclamation!

The Process

The initial encounter Moses had with the Lord God was the burning bush experience. An angel of the Lord appeared to him in a flame of a fire near a bush. The flaming angel in all its wonder did not consume the bush. Moses, being intrigued by this bush that was not consumed, went near to it. As Moses approached this bush, the Spirit of the Lord instructed him to remove his sandals because the ground was holy.

Once Moses did as the Lord instructed, the Lord God gave Moses a mandate. He was to deliver the children of Israel from being in captivity by the Egyptians. Moses was to lead the people to good land, a land flowing with milk and honey. The problem that proceeded next was belief. Moses did not have peace of mind about the instructions God had given him.

The misnomer about belief is that we place our apprehension on the thoughts of others. We tend to put statements like, "Who am I?" "What is His name?" "What shall I say to them?" "But suppose they will not believe me or listen to my voice?" "Suppose they say, the Lord has not appeared to you?" as Moses did, on others whom we are called to. Truth be told, those statements of doubt that we project on others are the manifestation of our lack of peace that has projected in our belief.

When Moses was instructed, he lacked the peace of mind knowing that God called him and instructed him for a massive task, such as delivering the children of Israel. With all your power, get to a place where you are not placing your doubts on the ones that are to receive you in some shape or form. If you are going to a business deal, try encouraging yourself with words like, "I will be favored," "They will receive me," and "I will close the deal," instead of saying doubtful things like, "What if I mess up?" "What if they don't like my pitch?" "What if I stutter?" These statements are for any given situation, whether you are closing a business deal, applying for a job, networking, or studying for an exam.

Evaluate your "I" statement and build confidence in what you are called to. Your thinking and your verbiage should be a positive affirmation—even if you do not believe it. As you continue to speak it, you are encouraging your spirit, and positive thinking will manifest in your heart. The key is to eliminate doubt. As you eliminate doubt, breathe forth positivity, possibilities, and God's perfect peace about yourself, your purpose, and your assignment. This is what God did with Moses until he got ahold of his peace.

Preparation

As Moses continued with doubt and his questions, God began to prepare him for his purpose. Before your proclamation, the preparation of your purpose will always take place behind closed doors. Moses needed to build his faith in the Lord so he could have peace about his purpose. Each and every time Moses questioned God about his task and purpose, God assured him that the assignment would be completed. Moses was not satisfied with the confirmations God gave him. So God performed a miracle in Moses's disbelief, to build his faith.

"So the Lord said to him, 'What is that in your hand?' He said, 'A rod'" (Ex. 4:2). God used what was in Moses's hand to give him peace about the purpose he would soon achieve. A small object like a rod is what built Moses's faith. After God asked that question, He then instructed Moses to cast the rod onto the ground. It turned into a serpent, and Moses ran. He was afraid, creeped out, and still unsure what God was doing in his life. Once the rod transformed into a snake, God told him to grab it by its tail! I don't know about you, but I'm not picking up a rod that transformed into a snake! You see, the Lord will use the foolish things that are in your possession, and what you already have authority over, to increase your stature.

After the first phase of preparation, it was time for God to proceed with the next. God dealt with his heart! The Lord God directed Moses to place his hand on his bosom! God was about to do an unthinkable and unimaginable act! Moses turned leprous as snow! In those days, a leper was considered a castaway, no good, a reject! If a leper was found, they were to be placed in isolation and away from the rest of the congregation!

As a leper, as someone who is in isolation, as someone who is a castaway, during your preparation phase, God is going to deal with the contents of your heart! As someone who is rejected by the masses, if you carry that rejection with you into your purpose, you could potentially abort your mission before it even starts. It was important that God transformed Moses into a leper. Moses dealt with a level of rejection, doubt, and insecurity. As an Egyptian by adoption and Hebrew by blood, Moses was bound to suffer from a level of identity confusion and rejection. When God transformed Moses into a leper, He healed him!

This transformational act was the very thing that reassured Moses in his purpose, his calling, and in who he was in the Lord! Moses learned he was more than enough during his time of being in preparation! He was able to obtain a peace of mind about what God had called and instructed him to do.

Proclamation

This bold man, walking in authority, though he stuttered, was walking with his head held high. He had a sense of peace about his purpose. Peace that only came from being behind closed doors with the Father. For moments and time on end, Moses fought and questioned with the Lord, but God fought back! God pressed Moses and prepared him for his purpose. Now is the time for proclamation! He barges into the pharaoh's door commanding him to let his people go. Only to be rejected and denied.

Had it not been for those moments behind closed doors, Moses would have walked away and whimpered. But he held on and continued with his demand. Moses knew his purpose, and nothing nor anyone was going to deter him from accomplishing his mission! Not even the Red Sea! Everything God prepared Moses for was everything Moses performed. From rejection to creating an act of miracle with a "simple" rod. God used everything Moses had, to fulfill his purpose.

There will be times in your life when you may feel a sense of inadequacy, and you may even question your purpose or assignment. However, have peace of mind knowing that if God has called you, he will process, prepare, and proclaim you for the very task that is at hand. Your gift of peace is equipped with purpose. Your gift of peace is also packed with armor, so let's tap into it!

Proclaim and Protect

Now that your belief has established you in the perfect peace of the Lord, it's time to use that peace to protect your purpose, your mission, and your heart! As mentioned before, peace is a form of armor. You are to shod your feet with the preparation of the gospel of peace. As you continue your mission or journey, remember your preparation. Always remind yourself of how God affirmed you time and time again. Remember your closed-door experience. There will be moments of doubt and moments of rejection, but hold firm to what God has placed in you.

The enemy does not want to see you walking in your best self, nor does he want you to know that you're more than enough, so he'll fight you. You will experience attacks, setbacks, and obstacles, but your gift of peace is supposed to protect and strengthen you. Peace does not mean that everything will be perfect, or in the world's "perfect peace."

Peace is knowing that against all the odds, God has called you and is using you for His glory.

Your peace, through the Word of God, is going to protect you as you're walking on purpose. Use it! Whenever you are faced with opposition, fight back with the Word of God and the Words He spoke over you. You've been through the preparation process, now, during the proclamation, it's up to you to sustain it! Your purpose matters. Know that you're more than enough, and grab your peace of armor and protect your purpose!

My Prayer

Heavenly Father, I ask that you grace your child with the perfect peace of the purpose and mission you have bestowed upon them. Lord, cover and protect them. Process, prepare, and proclaim them in their purpose. Affirm them that they are more than enough. Everything that they need is within reach. The rod in their hand will be used for your glory as they complete the mission you have assigned to them. Lord, cover them! In your Son Jesus's name I do pray, amen♥

Mission: Use the Word of God as your armor, and protect your peace, protect your purpose!

8 | Fulfillment

One thing I know to be true is this: *"In Him was life, and the life was the light of men."*

John 1:4

Fuel on Purpose

So, the biggest hindrance and setback is fulfillment. The lack of having a grip on your purpose is one of the main reasons why you may be dealing with issues of identity, self-love, joy, and peace. Every ounce of discontentment falls back on fulfillment. The fulfillment of one's purpose brings a sense of belonging and meaning and makes life worthwhile. Everyone, at some point in time, has asked the infamous question, "What on earth am I here for?"

We are on a constant quest of <u>finding contentment</u>, <u>seeking purpose</u>, and <u>mastering our purpose</u>. Our efforts are generated and shaped by these three concepts. Early on in life, we were always taught to measure ourselves by our status quo. "What do you desire to become when you grow up?" This question was asked numerous times. So much that the pressure of "becoming" created contentment issues as we sought and mastered our purpose. The real question is, what do you consider purpose? What fulfills you? What is it that makes life worth living for? What is your why?

Finding Contentment

With the help of social outlets and reality TV, finding contentment has become a hard concept for many to grasp. It seems as if everyone is #winning and #goals. However, no one shows the behind-the-scenes hardship, work, and preparation it takes. There are behind-the-scenes moments that many are not privy to. It just so happens that you only see the results of the behind-the-scenes preparation, for the "on-stage performance."

What you don't see is how many times an individual had to speak life and encouraging words back into themselves. What you don't know is how they tried to abort their purpose time and time again. Though it seems as if they're winning and #livingtheirbestlife, they are struggling to keep up with the pressure and demands that are associated with their calling.

There is a price to pay for purpose. Somehow their appearance makes it okay to create them as goals, instead of cracking down on your own goals.

Ask yourself, what do you consider fulfillment? Is it obtaining a vast bank account? Having a long list of followers? Or is it becoming the best version of yourself? Wherever you find fulfillment, that's where you'll find contentment. Your contentment is found in your purpose. However, as you travel the road to purpose, keep in mind that there's a difference between contentment and being comfortable.

<u>To Be Content</u>

Contentment, according to Dictionary.com, is "satisfaction; ease of mind." This means that whatever you put your hands on, you have satisfaction. Your purpose fulfilled gives you an ease of mind. When walking on purpose, you'll need the reassurance of knowing that you find satisfaction in what you are doing. During the course of fulfilling your purpose, contentment will come in handy. When trials, setbacks, and hardships associated with your destiny come, you'll be able to stand as the Apostle Paul was able to stand.

In Philippians 4, Paul confessed that whatever state he was in, he learned how to be <u>content</u>. He knew how to endure during the hardest times of his calling, and he knew how to rejoice during the graceful moments of his purpose. He knew that because he was a man walking on purpose, all his experiences, whether good or bad, had a purpose.

Paul understood the definition of finding contentment. He knew that the journey to fulfilling his purpose would not be an easy task, though it was rewarding. Whatever you consider purposeful, you must ask yourself, will you be able to stand and endure when your purpose doesn't quite feel like a calling? Will you be able to stand against being ridiculed and facing objection? Will you be able to keep your feet planted knowing that you're on a mission to your see your calling fulfilled?

To Be Comfortable

We all love the feeling of comfort. It's familiar, it's safe, and it's our go-to position. It's also what keeps us from growing forward. *Growth*, on the other hand, hurts. It stretches you, and it pushes you past the limits of where you were. Comfort says, while I'm currently in my ideal state, don't force me to my peak. I'm unsure of what's over the edge. It feels so good.

The problem with comfort is that it's deceiving. It gives the appearance that where you currently are is as good as it gets. Comfort does not give the option, the possibility, nor growth, a thought. It stunts your potential and keeps you at bay. Unfortunately, many individuals have no clue that they are bound by comfort. If they do, they're unsure of how to move forward. Let's spend a few moments understanding if you are bound, as well as unsticking you! This is vital. Should you ever get a hold of knowing that you're more than enough, you must move forward and get out of your comfort, so you can own your purpose.

Figuring out if you're bound is the easy part. Examine yourself. Have you been struggling with doubt, fear, or inadequacy? If so, those are indicators of comfort. When doubt, fear, and inadequacy seep in, they prevent you from owning you and growing into the person God destined you to become. All those traits stunt growth!

You also want to determine if you have any unfinished task, or unfilled goals or desires. Anything unfilled constitutes comfort of some form. Get in the habit of completing your task and finishing your missions. Believe that anything you put your hands to will flourish. If you have concerns about whether or not God will approve, you must try to find out. Without moving forward, you will never know if it's in God's will or not.

I'm aware that it may be hard to finish what you've started. Being stuck is no joke. Moving past that level of comfort is essential. You've started off strong, but somewhere along the line, you've lost hope and determination and are all together are unsure of your purpose, your direction, or what to do next. Just hit the reset button and determine how to evolve into the next phase. Perhaps your audience changed. As your audience changes, so should you. Figure out how to reinvent yourself.

Learn your target and increase your knowledge, skill, and confidence to match the direction you're going in.

Another factor you could incorporate when moving past the comfort level is motivating yourself. Regularly speak life into your purpose. Think of it like this: if you won't encourage yourself, who will? Remember, God, birthed purpose inside of you! It's your job to fulfill your calling. Know that you're more than enough. Everything you need to do precisely what God has called you to do is nestled right within your reach. All you must do is grab it!

Get into the position where you are content with your calling. Always make strides toward your purpose and toward being your best self yet. One tip I would add is to celebrate every achievement. Any step that is taken toward your goal, purpose, or calling must be acknowledged and celebrated. Now, you don't have to go all out. Acknowledge the steps that were taken and how far you've come. Pat yourself on the back. You're more than enough.

Seeking Purpose

Okay, darling, let's get to the nitty-gritty. Everything we've covered so far has prepared you for this divine moment: seeking purpose. From here on in, we'll cover mastering and sustaining your purpose. Each and every soul placed here on earth is here for an assignment of some sort. To broadly summarize it, your purpose is to fulfill the great commission of making disciples of all nations. This means, glorify God in all you do. As you glorify Him, you are making disciples by being an exemplary standard of Christ's conduct here on earth. Thus, in your nature, you are drawing souls to Christ.

How you classify your specific job description and what your duty entails is another determination. While we are placed to honor, serve, and lead souls to Christ, our mission will be fulfilled in our individualized purpose. The only way to honestly know what your divine purpose is on earth is to sit at the feet of the Father and seek Him. Allow Him to show you who you are in Him. God has a specific tailormade purpose that only you can achieve and one that only He can give.

I guarantee you, your purpose is already in your hand. The very thing you were created to do is already in your frontal. When God created you, He created you with a host of desires. Those desires are to be fulfilled in such a manner that will bring glory to Him. Many believe that when they come to Christ, they are to forget everything they ever did that was outside of him. On the contrary, that's not true. The way the Lord made you is the way He's going to use you! From the age of five, I loved doing hair. Little did I know, along with a host of other things, that love and desire is a part of my purpose.

Figure out what you are passionate about. Learn what drives you. Take your shot at you! Whatever it is that you love with your entire heart, to the point that you are willing to do it for free, that's where your purpose lies. Now, I'm not saying to give your gift with no return. No, read the parable of the talent in Matthew 25:14-30. Don't hide your passion, dream, or talent. Use it! Multiply it! Watch it grow exponentially and entrust God with it! When He sees that you've been faithful to what He has already given you, He'll bless you with more!

Mastering Purpose

So, the other day my friend asked what I normally do when I feel lonely. In all honesty, I had forgotten that I ever felt lonely. My response to her was, "Hone in on my purpose." I had no idea that the moment where I was driven in my purpose was where I would find contentment. I felt fulfilled, to the point that my inhibitions were not a factor. My faults, shortcoming, or lacks did not matter. I finally got to a place where I began mastering my purpose. Now, by any means, I have not arrived— I'm far from that. What I'm saying is, I have learned how to honor and dedicate my time and my energy to what God has planted inside of me. Thus, I am mastering my purpose.

Learning how to master your purpose will require you learning how to be content in seeking your purpose. Once you have an idea of what your purpose is, gun for it like it is nobody's business! Be intentional about refining what God has placed in you. All efforts should be centered around increasing your talents and bringing glory to the Father.

When it comes to increasing, this could mean studying your craft. Examine others who are walking in the same or similar lane as you. Figure out what their journey is like. Learn from their mistakes. In addition to studying, learn how to overcome barriers and setbacks. Build your skin and cut your teeth. Wet your feet a little, get in the game, and see what arena or audience your purpose will fall in.

Embrace your "now" season. Live in every moment and continue to evolve into the person God has destined for you. Make no apologies for your growth, maturity, or who you do and do not choose to hang around. Your purpose is far too important to allow flies, serpents, or distractions to keep you from moving forward. As a tip, continue to love yourself beyond measures. The moment you own you will be the moment you own and embrace every stage you are in when it comes to mastering your purpose!

Lastly, as you move closer to your purpose, protect it at all costs! As you walk on purpose, you are very vulnerable. You're open, and you're new. You must protect your purpose. This may mean keeping your mouth shut until you've developed your confidence to the point where you know you're not easily moved or shaken. Also, keep a few people in your corner who you know will motivate and push you! You'll need it!

My Prayer

Dear Heavenly Father, in the name of Jesus, Lord, I ask that you cover over your child and breathe in them a new wind. Give them hope and increase their desire to walk into their God-given purpose. Father, equip them with discernment as they move forward. Lord God, I ask all this in your Son Jesus's name, amen♥

Mission: Identify what you consider purposeful and go for it!

9 | Fire

One thing I know to be true is this: *"The bush was burning with fire, but the bush was not consumed."*

Exodus 3:2

Furnace to Refine

I remember it like it were yesterday. It felt as if I was losing my mind! I was battling with so many thoughts, and physically, I was having a hard time. Doubt, uncertainty, confusion, and a host of other ideas bombarded my mind. On top of that, I lost a ton of weight, my locks were thinning and falling out, and massive lumps were protruding from my scalp. It got so bad that going to the doctor was not an option, it was a mandate. If you know me, then you know going to the doctor is my absolute last resort.

There were tons of tests administered around that time. From a CT scan to vital testing, screening for cancer and lupus, along with a host of other exams. Never had I ever experienced a health scare like this. I was completely unsure if I was coming or going. All I knew was that something had taken place internally. It was hard for me to keep my peace. However, I was determined to figure out what was wrong.

While I anxiously waited for my test results, I fought hard to tap into the peace of Christ. However, I mustered the strength. I began prophesying over myself. I looked in the mirror and declared: "There is nothing wrong with you. Stop going to the doctors; they won't find anything! God is after you! He's after your identity, your purpose, and your heart!"

The Lord desires to take the box that you've placed Him in and tear it apart. He is going to catapult you into a new dimension. The Lord desires to take you higher, but first, you must go through the fire! Whew! After that intense prophecy, I was convinced I was going through a different-level attack. However, I was still unsure; after two weeks, I had not heard from the doctors.

I became a worrying mess! Without proper notice, I visited every physician I had seen. My thoughts were confirmed! There was absolutely nothing wrong with me! In fact, all the doctors thought I was completely insane, showing up at their offices uninvited. Their words were: "Armani, go home! I didn't call because every single one of your test results came back negative! Your vitals look amazing! You're perfectly healthy!" I couldn't understand. My thoughts were, if I was completely fine, then that only meant one thing.

I was in for one heck of a ride. God was dealing with me! Refining me and molding me for the next dimension I was walking in! It was more than a spiritual attack; it was a spiritual acceleration! I was not to privy to this shift. While it seems all fine and dandy to be catapulted in a new direction, it's not a pleasurable encounter. I wrote a blog about my experience, which I'll share at the end of this chapter.

There comes a time when God is going to place you through the fire. The fire is not favorable whatsoever! It burns, it's uncomfortable, it's uncommon, and it's the road less traveled. However, should you desire to grow in the Lord, the fire is needed! In fact, the fire is inevitable.

Into the Furnace You Go!

Many of us know the story of Daniel and the three Hebrew boys. The story is amazing! It details a fantastic testimony of being able to stand the test of time and objectify the very thing that is trying to turn you away from what you believe in. In fact, I'll share with you in detail how Daniel and the three Hebrew boys stood the test of time and were refined through their obedience.

According to Daniel 1–3, it was the third year of the reign of Jehoiakim, King of Judah, when Nebuchadnezzar, King of Babylon, came to Jerusalem and captured it! Once Nebuchadnezzar got a hold of this territory, he sent a decree to gather some noble, good-looking, gifted, and knowledgeable young men of Israel. He desired to train them and use them as servants in his palace. The young men were only to eat and drink what they were told to. This included a selection of the king's delicacies and wine.

Though it was a decree for all to eat of the king's delicacies and drink of his wine, Daniel and his friends decided against it. Daniel made the decision not to defile himself with the king's food. He didn't want to be bound by his dictates nor ruled by his gods. Due to Daniel making a stand not to defile himself with the king's selection, God favored him. When Daniel was questioned about such objection, they permitted Daniel to eat and drink as he pleased, which was vegetables and water. However, there was one provision: Daniel and his friends were going to be tested for ten days. For the king to honor Daniel's request, they had to ensure that the boys would remain healthy while eating only veggies and drinking water.

After the completion of the ten days, the appearance of Daniel and his friends was much healthier than the appearance of those who had eaten of the king's food. As a result, Daniel and the three Hebrew boys were not required to eat of the king's delicacies. Because of their obedience and tenacity, God increased Daniel and his friends in knowledge, skills in all literature, and wisdom. He endowed them. In addition to that, God gave Daniel a portion of visions and dream interpretation.

Once the years of training and preparation was up, all the young men went before the king. The king wanted to select from them those whom he could entrust as his servants. Luckily, since the Lord endowed the boys, they were favored in the sight of the king. Daniel and His friends were selected to serve in the king's palace. We all know that the king has a way of driving his demands on the people he's governing.

Just like with the food, the king gave an order for all to worship and bow down to his gods. Coincidentally, this was not Daniel's first rodeo. Once again, he objected to such an act. He was not going to bow down to foreign gods. His will and desires were to honor the Lord God with his entire life. In conjunction with the king creating a demand for all to worship his gods, he issued an order for those who refused to be sent into a fiery furnace. He wanted the objectors to die!

When it came down to the final verdict of whether Daniel and his crew would be sent into the furnace, Daniel held firm. He stated he would not bow down at any cost.

Should God save them, it would be good, Glory be to God. Should the Lord God choose not to save them, Glory be to God! Whatever outcome Daniel and His friends were to receive, Daniel was <u>content in his purpose</u>. Daniel and his friends were sentenced to the furnace, which was set to the maximum heat. Daniel and his friends went into the furnace, untouched. Not a hair on their head was scorched. Not even the stench of fire was detected. Most importantly, they didn't come out of the furnace alone. The Spirit of the Lord accompanied Daniel and his friends.

The Inevitable Mandate

There comes a point in time when the Lord God will examine and test you. The Lord is seeking to see how rooted you are. He wants to determine whether you'll sink or swim. Will you remain planted as a tree when waters get too high? Or, will you fall with the waves and lose your footing? Most of the time, the Lord tests you for two reasons: when it's time to refine and perfect what you've learned and experienced (like quizzes), or when you've learned all you needed to learn on your current level, and it's time to elevate or proceed to the next assignment (like the final exam).

Going back to content versus comfort, it's essential that you understand what it means to be content and not remain comfortable and stagnant. Growth is inevitable; embrace the fire as the three Hebrew boys. Like me, you may go through one heck of a war, but it may be necessary. Being refined and being elevated is always desirable. Everyone wants to be promoted and proceed to the next phase of life and purpose. So everyone must experience their share of being refined through the fire. This is not to say that everyone will experience the same level of persecution, hardship, or warfare. This is to say that everyone will experience some degree of discomfort as growth takes place.

Refine to Perfect

When it comes to perfecting, the Lord uses everything you've ever studied, learned, and experienced to strengthen you in your stature. Just like my example of me praying for patience. I underwent numerous levels of being placed in the fire, to reinforce and perfect me in the fruit of patience. You may experience the same thing. As you do, the Lord is looking for any impurities that may be nestled within you. Those impurities cannot grow with you. Therefore, you must be placed into the fire of some sort.

Think of it as gold. When gold is found, like you, it already has some form, shape, and stature. However, though there's substance, in its original state, it's not perfected. When you come to Christ, you have some knowledge and some substance in Him. However, you are not totally refined or completely perfected in Him. Therefore, for your current season, you must be perfected. As you've grown in Christ and obtained an ample amount of knowledge and wisdom, you may not be completely ready to issue what you've learned until you've been refined to perfection. Like school, though you've taken the class, you will not proceed to your next level until you've mastered your final exam.

What Setting Do You Prefer?

Everyone loves gold. However, if you were to take a page out of "gold's" book, you would gladly decline. During the refining process, gold, in its purest form, is placed into extreme heat. The desire is to remove the impurities. Before eliminating impurities, samples are taken to see what level, degree, and process the gold must be placed in. Should you go in the correct direction and grow properly, the Lord will examine and test your level before the extreme heat.

As for Daniel and his friends, the Lord had already tested them. The Lord knew what heat they could endure. They had proven themselves; therefore, the maximum heat was administered. They chose not to conform; they decided to be set apart. They decided to stand firm in the Lord. Ask yourself, are you conforming when you're supposed to be set apart? Have you fallen victim to the pressure, or will you stand the test of time knowing that you're living for the Lord?

For the Lord to know what degree to turn the heat on, He'll test your heart, mind, and ability to stand in Him. These tests are minor. They are subtle attacks but useful. They're packed with just the right amount of punch, to the point that you'll be able to learn from your errors and mistakes. The key is to keep you on your toes, to keep you in position long enough so you can grow forward and proceed to the next round of testing.

Careful, should you fail to pass or learn from your exams, you'll continue to go through the same repetitive cycle until you've learned and are refined in your current level. This means you'll experience the same form of attacks, warfare, and battles over and over again. It will feel as if God has forgotten about you. But He hasn't. He wants to strengthen you. He wants you to learn and grow from your season. Failure to understand that will keep you in your current position, not moving forward into the next phase.

Typically, test and trials are according to seasons, so you must pass an exam or get through the current fire prior to entering the next season. Daniel and the three Hebrew boys went through a season where they had to stand firm in the Lord. That season prepared them for the fire that was to come. Perhaps recently you've been through a season where you had to perfect your heart in love. Each test you've encountered could be centered around you developing in loving yourself and loving others.

This means you may be placed in situations where it's not easy to love on others for some reason or another. Perhaps this time around you may even feel as if you've gone too far from God and there's no way you could forgive yourself. Or could it be that you're struggling with seeing your worth. Whatever it may be, the Lord will administer tests that are compatible with your current season. As a tip for the wise, always expect your quizzes to be centered around your current season. Just like a professor, God won't quiz you on anything you haven't learned. Unless it's a bonus question where He wants to prepare you for the next season.

Refine and Elevate

So, the next phase of refining gold is to turn up the heat. Heat is used to separate the impurities. Or, when it comes to administering tests, bonus questions are used to separate your prior knowledge to prepare you for the next level. As gold is being refined, there is constant shifting that is taking place. This shifting is to remove the impurities. Shifting is also taking place within the fire. As the Lord is placing you in the fire, through intense tests and trials, there's always shifting involved.

This shifting is to separate, remove, and eliminate the factors in your life that are currently keeping you from being in your perfected state. This shifting could be a shift in your thinking. The Lord could be changing your mindset, your heart, and your thoughts about His glory and the people that are centered around you. This shifting could also be eliminating individuals and environments that are not supposed to go with you into the next realm.

It's important to understand that shifting is a part of elevation. Just as impurities are not permitted in the final stage of gold, neither is what the Lord is shifting from you. There will be thinking and mentalities that are not allowed. Kingdom living requires Kingdom mindset. As you are being elevated, your frame of mind will be perfected. The people you hold close to you may be removed. Some individuals are not permitted in your current season. Let them go! Don't allow your trap thinking or people bondage keep you from entering your next phase.

During elevation, there will be higher requirements. You're held to a higher degree. What you used to do, and get away with, will not be tolerated. You should be at the point where you're not falling victim to conformity nor are you wavering with small winds. The Lord has used the minor test and the slight winds to prepare you so your feet can remain planted. Now is the time when heavy winds will blow in your direction.

<u>So, about This Phase</u>

Those heavy winds are to continue to increase your posture and your roots that are in Him. It's your responsibility to ensure that they remain rooted. This will require an increasing level of fervent prayer and fasting, and more of you crucifying your flesh. Just like with small winds, should you fail a test, you'll continue in the same circle until you've conquered what the Lord wants you to overcome. So, continue to hold fast and reject doubting thoughts that are keeping you from growing forward.

Keep in mind, your elevation is not only for you. Others are connected to your elevation. Therefore, it's important to detach from individuals and environments that have no place in your future. Failure to do so will sabotage your process and damage the surge that's connecting you to those you are called to. Some things are better at keeping you at bay than accelerating you.

This area of growth is lonesome, and you're also pouring out more than you're getting back. And that's okay. Now is when you connect strength to the Lord. As you are being refined for elevation, you'll have to learn that the Lord is your source. You're in a crucial time of your life where your future depends and relies on your connection to the Father. You must hold onto your peace knowing that every test, trial, and attack that comes your way is to strengthen and elevate you for the next phase and dimension.

Stand the Test of Time

The beautiful thing about being tested is that as you overcome your tests, you grow from them. You conquer them in such a way that you now you have dominion over those areas of attack. So when those attacks, tests and trials, or fires get too hot, you're aware. Well, you're supposed to be apprised of them. You're supposed to use what you've learned and experienced for the next level you'll be entering.

Nothing you endure, overcome, and go through will be in vain. The Lord will use everything for your good . . . if you're called by Him and love Him. He'll use all your trials for a higher purpose than you've ever imagined. I want to encourage you: as you go through your test and the fire, remain planted. Ask the Lord for discernment. Ask Him for wisdom. Wisdom is needed. You'll need to have an idea if the Lord is putting you through the fire to refine you or putting you through the fire because you've strayed. I'm not going to talk much about going astray here, but do know that when you've gone outside of God's will, you will experience some level of attack, and it may even feel as if you're going through the fire. So keep that in mind and continue to remain in prayer!

Good luck! Remain planted and firm in His will and His purpose!

My Testi-Blog (Testimony Formed into a Blog)

For your knowledge, this testimony is told in four parts: Virtue, Comfort, Me, and God. *Virtue* is whom God called me to be. *Comfort* is the complacency that refused to move. *Me* was me being stuck at a crossroads. I desired to grow and become this virtuous woman, but being comfortable was also a safety net. And *God*, well, His voice was loud and clear. He was watching me every moment of the way. Keep in mind this is only a glimpse of my experience.

As Told by *Virtue:*

She should have known I was coming after her. It was only a matter of time before we were in a collision. There was no way she could carry the *Comfort* of her past into being this *Virtue*. Of a woman, she even admits that the moment her pastor preached, it seemed as if there was no one else in the room, with the exception of God. It was as if He wanted to pry open the barriers of what she buried. So, she hid it.

She didn't know; she thought she was only going to acknowledge the hidden secrets and keep it moving. She had no idea that God was going to have me confront them, head-on, forcing a Holy collision of two worlds, colliding into a supernatural atomic bomb. She didn't know. She walked out of church, the following weeks and months, thinking everything was okay and the battle was over. Little did she know the ground He wanted to sow into was being tended to—plowed and ripped apart. The foundation she once believed in, obliterated. The only way I can describe it is as a *Holy collision*.

Just imagine, wanting to walk into the virtue of a woman you are called to be, yet stuck in the comfort of your past. There's no way the two can reside; one must GO. I no longer wanted to be the pretentious imagination of her potential. I wanted to become her, all of her. Too many lives are attached to the purpose and plan God has for her, so I had to annihilate the world she was living in. She was comfortable, and that was the problem, so I confronted her. She must understand that to become the virtue of THIS woman, she must let go of her comfort and embrace the uncomfortable.

As Told by *Comfort:*

I wonder if someone can see me screaming, panicking, crying for help. I turn to God, but the silence from His mouth is eerie. I'm not used to this. I feel as if I'm optional, and it almost seems as if my time is running out. I want to scream, but I'm afraid. Will my *vulnerability* tell on me? Will my secrets be revealed? Better yet, I think I have a solution. I can put on a better façade. I know the scriptures well. I mean, I can preach, but do I really have to live it out? I know God said He'd make all things new, but does that include me? It can't be.

If I hold on a little while longer, I can fix this. It can be as if I erased it, though I've suppressed it. She doesn't need to confront it. She should ignore this area a little while longer. If I keep quiet, *fear* just might go away. I don't want conflict; she can walk in silence and eventually this might disappear. Magically *insecurities* might turn into victories and then . . . I can finally walk confidently. Right?

Why can't she fiercely walk for the Lord and not worry about the hidden truths? Oh, how I wish that were possible . . . Who would have thought that the contents of what I buried so well would appear during a time such as this? I thought I'd done such a great job masking fear, hurt, and insecurities. It seems as if the purposed me is confronting the very root of me. However, the comfort of this identity does not want to reveal my vulnerabilities. Oh, how the spirit and the flesh are at enmity, causing a collision of things.

As Told by *Me*:

Hey, it's me. Imagine, waking up in the middle of a battlefield, not realizing just nights before you declared war. I thought it was only a small prophecy while I was looking in the mirror declaring things. I had no idea the

Virtue of me, spoke to the Comfort of me. She took charge with full authority. She told her, *God was after the secret things. God was after the very image of me.* I thought I was just affirming me. Little did I know, I paved a way for my two worlds to collide. A catastrophe. God wanted to wreck all of me. I wanted to let Him. I was afraid.

I've lived so long in this shell that I've formed. I created an identity that I thought fit me perfectly. I had no idea that I couldn't take this mask with me. Sure, God enlisted me. I planned to lug this false identity, but God stopped me and showed me the REAL ME. She's packed powerfully, originally how God intended me to be. She didn't carry a mistaken identity, she was sure and confidently walked in authority. As I looked back, I saw shrunken me, afraid of her date with destiny. She knew her time was up; it was only a matter of manifesting physically. I was ready for these two worlds to meet. I was excited to become all that God intended me to be.

HOWEVER! I've been in spiritual battles numerous times, but no one told me that this one, concerning identity, was going to be a fight that would wreck me. My friend told me to be ready, but I don't even think she knew what was in store for me. I'm screaming out for God to help me, but He's silently watching me, searching the inner parts of me. If you ask me, I feel as if I'm being stretched beyond capacity. It's like there are two parts of me: one walks in authority, the other in timidity. And then there's me. The person everyone sees, trying to walk confidently as if Galatians 5:17 is not being fulfilled within me. The flesh and the Spirit are warring inside me, so much that it's affecting me physically. I've lost a head full of hair, and my weight is constantly changing. My skin, well . . . that's beyond me, but these headaches and chest pains are killing me. Then I hear . . .

<u>God's Voice</u>

Let me speak. Don't dare think for one second I have left thee. I will be with thee: for I have said, "I will not fail thee nor forsake thee." But you lied to me. You said you gave me your whole heart, but you kept something from me. I'm after what you've hidden from me.

Your very purpose is buried in your identity, so I must reshape thee. What you're going through is for the purpose I have given you. You're going to bear much fruit, so I must keep pruning you. Continue to abide in ME, and I will comfort thee.

Yes, I know this is affecting you physically, but you must trust Me. Stop going to the doctors; they can't see what I see spiritually. Don't worry, I'm fixing everything. You've lost hair because thou needest thy crown placed properly. And thou weight, I'm increasing thee. Your skin will glow as if you're bathing in milk and honey. Your chest is killing thee because I'm turning your heart back toward me—completely. And those headaches, don't worry, they'll be gone shortly; that false image you've created is at enmity with me. Think of it as the parable of the wineskins. I cannot pour new anointing into your old flesh. Otherwise, you will burst. For you don't have the capacity to bear what I am pouring into thee. For this new wine I am giving thee requires a new wineskin. Fear not, for I am reshaping thee.

<u>My Prayer:</u>

Dear Heavenly Father, Lord, I pray that you cover and grace your child. Father, equip them and sustain them as they grow forward in you! Lord, walk with them as they proceed into tests and trials. Holy Spirit covers them in Jesus's name. Lord God, I ask all this in your Son Jesus's name, amen♥

<u>Mission:</u> Remain planted and wait on the Word of God. Remember to stand, even in the midst of a fiery storm.

10 | You're More Than Enough

One thing I know to be true is this: *"For I know the thoughts that I think toward you, says the Lord, thoughts of peace and not of evil, to give you a future and a hope."*
Jeremiah 29:11

Home Stretch

You are almost there! Before we close out, I do want to encourage you in a few more pointers. 1. Fight 2. Uplift 3. Share. These three concepts are embedded within the entire command that Christ gave us for making disciples and loving on him. Should we look closely, we'll be able to see that these three are all working together as you fulfill your purpose and walk in the ultimate mission of Christ, all while keeping and staying true to your identity.

Firefighter

Oh, you thought we were finished talking about fire? Yeah, naw, we're not! We only had the entree; now it's time for the best part. The dessert! Yummy! So, let's get to it! When it comes to being a firefighter, you are someone who fights fire! However, you don't just fight fire for yourself. You fight fires for others. If you just so happen to have a fire of your own, you have the tools, so you'll know what to do!

<u>Toolbox</u>

The Bible tells us that we overcome by the blood of the lamb and the word of our testimony (Rev. 12:11). It further goes to state that they did not love their lives, not even unto death. As a firefighter, you fight fires, even if it means risking your life in some way. You go in headfirst, going to war to put out the blaze. As a firefighter for Christ, you go in headfirst going to war for anyone. You intercede, you assist, you give them your hand, pray for them, and disciple them. You stand right next to them and help them fight for their lives just as Christ has fought for your life.

The Lord God desires us to be in partnership with the Holy Spirit as we stand in the gap for those who are either in unbelief or struggling with their walk. It's our ultimate purpose as stated in the Great Commission found in Matthew, to make disciples and baptize them in Jesus's name. By default, you are a firefighter, and your toolbox is the armor of God. Your toolbox is your name. Your toolbox is your faith, your belief, your love, and your peace. Your toolbox is found in your identity. It'll be, hard, nearly impossible, to fully and adequately fight fires for others if you lack the understanding and knowledge of your name, identity, and purpose.

As a firefighter who is enlisted in the army of God, you must know who you are; you must understand your power and purpose, you must know you're more than enough. You are a firefighter. Your fighting doesn't end when the fire is put out. Your fight is on a continual basis. Continually, I pray for my loved ones and those who are not in Christ. After I've seen the manifestation of my fervent prayer, I keep fighting. I know should they continue to walk in the Lord and walk in purpose, on purpose, my continual efforts are needed to fill in the gap. Your constant efforts are required, and not a single prayer or fast will go in vain. So keep fighting.

Your fighting may mean that as you sow and push others, you are sowing and pushing yourself so you *can* push others. Fighting for others is not easy; it's time-consuming and at times draining, but it's worth it! A significant measure is to continually fuel yourself on the Word and will of God. Be mindful as a firefighter; you are fighting in an unseen realm. So your waring is entirely in the supernatural. It's done on earth which is done in heaven, and your work in the spiritual realm will manifest itself on earth and in the lives you are fighting for, according to God's timing.

By fulfilling the great commission, you are making disciples. You make disciples by fighting for people's salvation and partnering with the Holy Spirit as you lead them to Christ. He then baptizes them in His Holy Spirit!

Lifting as You Climb

Your fighting is called *lifting as you climb*. When you're up, never kick someone when they're down. Give them your hand and help them reach. There will be times when you may need that same hand, to help you reach. We all fall short of the glory of God, we all are in desperate need of a savior and of some good fixing. So, as you climb and make your way to the top of your purpose, your identity, and the perfect will of God, look down and not back. Give your lending hand and lift, as you climb.

Often, many are intimidated and are afraid to lift when they climb. They feel as if, should they do so, they will lose something, they will get looked over, or perhaps the person they've helped will either surpass them or forget them in their process. The truth of the matter is, that is not your concern. One plants and another waters. It just so happens that God may be using you to either plant or water. But it's the Lord that brings the increase. Which means, no one can ever take anything from you that they did not add to you! It's Christ that brings the increase.

Sure, along the process of lifting and helping others, you may get burnt and feel unappreciated. I know, I've been there! But you'll grow to learn and realize that it's in your human nature to lift as you climb, so nine times out of ten, you probably won't be able to help it. Embrace it! As you do, know that it's God that brings the increase, and it's God that rewards you. Your treasure will be stored in heaven.

<u>Exponentially Share</u>

Sharing is caring. Don't stop until your heart does (sorry). Even after that, you'll continue to share. Your legacy is in what you've shared, what you've contributed, what you've done with your talents, time, gifts, and fruit. You may not get a plaque, podium, award, or any grand recognition. But as you get, give, and more will be given to you. You are a firefighter, which means you have something to give to others that will be beneficial and useful to them.

By fulfilling the great commission, you are making disciples. You make disciples by fighting for their salvation, partnering with the Holy Spirit as you lead them to Christ, and then baptizing them in His Holy Spirit! Those same disciples, you are lifting as you climb your way to the top of your purpose ladder. No one ever truly makes it until it's time for the "horn" to blow. So why not lift as you climb? By doing so, you are not just making disciples; you are making disciples exponentially. You're firefighting, and your lifting is an example to those who are watching you—they will follow. You are a living testimony, so continue to allow your light to shine and live in a glorious light for the Lord. Know that every experience, every lift, every fire that you've put out, is for the glory of God, and He is using it for your purpose.

Until Next Time

<u>All Things Are Working Together</u>

Ironically, as I began writing this book, just when I was about to affirm myself, my mother walked into my room and led me to my full-length mirror. She asked me what I saw, and to call out my beauty and my flaws for what they were (packaged perfectly). Excitedly, I did. "Child, you're beautiful!" Little did she know I had just finished my intro where I told the story of the young girl who could not identify herself as beautiful, let alone *more than enough.*

But she finally said her name. My name is *beautiful*, and I identify with Jesus Christ as my Lord and Savior who thinks I'm more than enough. In fact, He thought I was to die for. He thought you were to die for! You're More Than Enough.

You're more than enough, so embrace your covering, whether parental or spiritual. The people God has put in your life are there to guide and to nurture you whole. As you're being nurtured whole, you're also getting full knowledge of your identity in Christ. It's essential to know that you're more than enough than to walk around being masked and marked and not knowing your full identity or purpose. Do remember that it's okay to love yourself wholeheartedly. As you increase yourself in love, prepare yourself for love by patiently waiting.

My darling, continue to rest assured and know that you're more than enough. Christ thought you were to die for. He came so you can have joy and joy abundantly. His desire for you is to live life in the best form possible, all while giving glory and praise to Him. No longer will you walk around with a countenance that the world gives. But you will rest assured, knowing that Christ came bearing gifts so you can flourish in Him. Gifts such as peace, which is not only a gift but a fruit, and His armor. This gift is to prepare and equips you as you walk in purpose and walk in Him.

The Lord God knows that should you walk in the fullness of Him and in what He calls you to walk into, you must be equipped with His glory so you can fulfill your calling and purpose here on earth. It's His will that you're His glory carrier and are aware of His glory that is on your life. The walk to fulfilling your purpose is not an easy one. There will be many test trials and "fires," so to speak. These various tribulations are not to shake you, but to help catapult you into being your best self as you increase this journey to knowing that you're more than enough.

Most importantly, your ultimate purpose is to make disciples, which is pouring back out what was poured into you. Everything that you've learned, experienced, and encountered can now be used for those who are rising after you. Continue to fight fires for them and lift them. Remember, don't kick them; know that as you give, more will be given to you. Now is the time to share your story; share your purpose and your knowledge with others whom may need it. You never know what miracle, life, or dream will be ignited due to your tenacity and obedience. Your voice and purpose matters, so use it! I know I am.

You Have Everything It Takes

My dear, I don't want you to think that you're ill-prepared. But instead, know that you are clothed with everything you need to sustain your purpose, integrity, and walk as you fulfill the will of God. You have that and more, all while staying true to the very identity that God gave you. Your name is your ticket! So never, ever let anyone or anything formulate a name other than that which was given to you. Now, you've been with me for ten chapters plus and the acknowledgments and the Intro, so by now, you know that I'm not talking about your government name. I'm talking about your purpose name!

You're More Than Enough. Should you forget anything that we've discussed, remember that and own your purpose! Once we leave here, for now, you're on your own. That is, until we meet again. And, my friend, we will meet again! But as you wait, hold fast and continue to meditate on His Words. Daily! In Christ is your identity. In Christ is your purpose. In Christ, there's hope and a future. Until next time, Stay Blessed, Stress Less, Read Your Bible!

My Prayer

Dear Heavenly Father, I pray that you bring all things to remembrance. Show your child that they are more than enough and they have everything they need to fulfill their ultimate purpose. Father, I ask that you continue to embrace your child and to push and assist them in walking boldly in you! In Jesus's name I do pray, amen ♥

Mission: Know that You're More Than Enough. Allow God to do the work in you as you walk toward owning your purpose!

Closing

Let's Make It Practical

Oh, wait! Come here! You thought we were finished? Not quite, almost. I didn't want you to leave without your goodie bag! So sit tight!

<u>What's in the Bag</u>

So, in this bag are ten practical tips that will help you sustain your identity, purpose, and confidence:

1. Meditate on the Word of God. In His Word are your identity, your purpose, and your fuel.

2. I have a prayer wall. Use your house and wherever you frequently are as a covering. Cover your environment with the Word of God. (Perhaps, like mine, it is a wall.)

3. I have millions of journals. Journals are great for documenting your growth, journey, and steps taken in your purpose. Create or purchase a journal that you can use to notate every step or detail that you find to be beneficial to your life. Remember, celebrate every victory!

4. Fellowship! Get involved in a Bible-teaching church. Be engaged in a Christ-centered organization. Rise Ministry, Inc. is a great place for growth and developing in your purpose and becoming the leader that you are: www.RiseMinistry.Org.

5. Be intentional. Living in the fullness of your purpose and calling starts with you. You must have the determination to start and to become.

6. Love and give grace. Know that we all are living in a perfectly imperfect world. So give grace whenever you can.

7. Search and find. As you search for your purpose and identity, know that it will be found. Have the faith and determination to match your drive and desires.

8. Don't hold on. Never hold onto a grudge. Holding a fault hinders your growth and your ability to love and live the life of Christ so desired for you.

9. Learn to live!! While there is still life, live it! Enjoy it and learn to live your life to the fullness of Christ.

10. Honor the Lord Thy God, which is the first commandment given to you! Everything you do should be done to honor and exalt the Father which is in Heaven.

Mission: Encourage your friends to purchase this book! Connect with Rise Ministry, Inc. and leave us feedback about this book!

Definitions:

Chapter 5 – Joy, Page 74

1. Mending. 2018. In Dictionary.*com*. Retrieved May 8, 2018, from http://www.dictionary.com/browse/mending

Chapter 8 – Fulfillment, Page 103

1. Contentment. 2018. In Dictionary.*com*. Retrieved May 8, 2018, from http://www.dictionary.com/browse/contentment?s=t

Let's Connect!

www.RiseMinistry.org

ContactRiseMinistry@gmail.com

Facebook/Instagram @ RiseMinistryInc

Stay Blessed, Stress Less, Read Your Bible!

XoXo,

Armani White

www.ingramcontent.com/pod-product-compliance
Lightning Source LLC
Chambersburg PA
CBHW050643160426
43194CB00010B/1785